ORDEAL BY CONCORDANCE

ORDEAL BY CONCORDANCE

An Historical Study of a Recent Literary Invention

BY

CONRAD HENRY MOEHLMAN

1955
Longmans Green & Co.
NEW YORK · LONDON · TORONTO

LONGMANS, GREEN AND CO., INC.
55 FIFTH AVENUE, NEW YORK 3

LONGMANS, GREEN AND CO. Ltd.
6 & 7 CLIFFORD STREET, LONDON W 1

LONGMANS, GREEN AND CO.
20 CRANFIELD ROAD, TORONTO 16

ORDEAL BY CONCORDANCE

PUBLISHED SIMULTANEOUSLY IN THE DOMINION OF CANADA
BY LONGMANS, GREEN AND CO., TORONTO

FIRST EDITION

LIBRARY OF CONGRESS CATALOG CARD NUMBER 55-11448

Printed in the United States of America
VAN REES PRESS • NEW YORK

TO CAROL

without whose encouragement, suggestions, patience, and typewriter this study could not have been completed.

CONTENTS

FOREWORD

THE strange story narrated in *Ordeal by Concordance* is concerned particularly with three documents: the twelve-page essay entitled "The Metaphysical Religion of Hegel," the title page with an "N.B." allegedly written by Mary Baker, and an odd, confused, and confusing covering letter allegedly composed by Francis Lieber and addressed to "Mr. Hiram Crafts, Secretary of Kantian Society, Boston Lyceum."

In 1936, the essay was published in a book by Walter M. Haushalter, entitled *Mrs. Eddy Purloins from Hegel.*[1] The thesis defended by the authors or editors of this volume comes to this:

The manuscript on *The Metaphysical Religion of Hegel* proves to be a lengthy and learned treatise in the handwriting of Lieber, bearing his signature and his pen name Christian Herrmann.[2]

There are these errors in the claim: The essay is not lengthy or learned or in the handwriting of Francis Lieber. It was not signed by him or composed by him. His pen name was not Christian Herrmann.

The alleged date of the essay is 1865 and of the copy, April, 1866. The manuscript must actually be dated at least decades later than this.

The essay was allegedly sent to "Mr. Hiram Crafts, Secretary of Kantian Society, Boston Lyceum." There never was a Kantian Society, Boston Lyceum, and the voluminous correspondence of

Francis Lieber shows no letter from Crafts to Lieber or from Lieber to Crafts.[3]

The essay is allegedly Hegelian: "The newly discovered Source Document, a deeply thoughtful philosophic discussion of Hegelianism by a German-American." [4]

No Hegelian scholar consulted agreed with this claim.

"This remarkable essay ... proves to be a manuscript of 8,200 words ... The Lieber Manuscript gains distinction as one of the most notable documents in the history of American Letters ..." [5]

In the editor-author's transcription of the essay, pages 71 to 112, our count yielded only 6,786 words, with only about 2,000 words Hegelian quotations! The contents proved to be a conflation from alleged Hegelian quotations, a dozen additional German and other writers, plus heavy borrowing from *Science and Health with Key to the Scriptures* by Mary Baker Eddy mostly from post-1875 editions.

The editor-author further claims that Mr. Crafts late in 1866 permitted Mrs. Eddy to hold and handle the "Lieber" essay. She allegedly made a copy of that essay, used it as basis for the First Edition of *Science and Health* and thereafter continued to use it, *especially in the last edition.*

But of the approximately 2,000 words quoted from Hegel on pages 71 to 112 of the editor's book, there are no parallels from the First Edition. Indeed, in the 206 quotes of the 121 references which the editor cites to prove dependence of Mrs. Eddy in these same pages, only one is listed as from the First Edition and *that proves to be from the inventor of the essay and not from Hegel.* Hegel is very conspicuous by his total absence from the First Edition of *Science and Health* in these quotations.

It is also alleged that Mrs. Eddy wrote the "N.B." on the title page of the essay.

Even an amateur in handwriting may produce reasons to raise doubts that the signature is in her handwriting.

The editor-author also alleges that *Christian Science* is Hegelianism when he is not alleging that it is dependent upon Fichte. That claim covers too much ground to begin with and will be demonstrated to be in error.

The editor-author presents the rambling covering letter as authentic. It is filled with inconsistencies and false claims.

On page 14 of his book, the editor-author remarks that "the fact is irrefutable that the chief doctrinal points, the main ideas in *Science and Health*, including the major portion of the 'Scientific Statement of Being' are appropriated verbatim from this antecedent statement, the newly discovered Source Document."

But the "Source Document" is not Hegelian, Mrs. Eddy did not use it, her system is not Hegelianism, and the editor's dogmatic assertion seems based upon a faulty use of concordance-method and of homiletical rather than historical, scientific procedure.

The editor-author by his own statements admits that his study is based upon the use of Christian Science concordances and, when they fail him, he cannot find his references, for example:

The Concordances to her writings show to what extraordinary extent the Lieber Document has been utilized.[6]

... as 54 interesting references to it in the Concordances testify.[7]

The Concordances reveal some 340 references to "idea" and "ideal."[8]

Reference to the Concordances reveal Fichte's idea of Ego-God incorporated throughout Mrs. Eddy's writings.[9]

All foot-note quotations, unless otherwise stated, are from the current edition of Science and Health.[10]

[Why? one asks. The answer is that out of 206 quotes from *Science and Health*, pp. 72 to 112, he apparently lists but one from the First Edition! He has no Concordance for the First Edition.] [11]

The reader should also bear in mind that the *Facsimile Reproduction of the Lieber Manuscript and of the Letter to Hiram Crafts* which appears after page 128 of the Haushalter book is according to a statement printed in 1947 apparently only "one-third size, roughly printed copy of photostat."

At the present time the three "Lieber" documents are in the custody of the Princeton Theological Seminary Library. The leaves are written on one side and measure about 10 by 14 inches of written lines.

On the various pages of the essay and of the covering letter there appears a kind of "bookkeeping" ruling, more or less clear. The title page in the photostat seems to be minus this ruling.

The numbering of the three documents—covering page, title page, and essay—begins only on page 2 of the essay and continues to page 12.

The numeral "1" of the dateline of the covering letter has been identified as "April 1" and "April 7." The "7" of the essay paging as well as the "1"s in pages "10," "11," "12" seem to demand April 1 as the intended date of the covering letter as do the omission of the day of the month in both the note below the subscription on page 12 and on the title page, in "April 1866."

To simplify reference to the three documents involved, "covering letter" will refer to the letter allegedly written in April, 1866, to "Mr. Hiram Crafts, Secretary of Kantian Society, Boston Lyceum" by "Francis Lieber"; "N.B." to the note allegedly written by Mrs. Eddy on the title page; and " 'Lieber' essay" to the twelve-page principal document entitled "The Metaphysical Religion of Hegel by Francis Lieber—'Christian Herrmann.' "

The names omitted from the "facsimile reproduction of letter and manuscript," [12] were recovered from the photostat of the original. The reason for their omission was given as:

In both the photographic and printed reproduction of the letter Dr. Lieber sent to Crafts along with the paper he had laboriously prepared to be read before the Kantian Society, blanks appear where certain names have been omitted. The omission has been made in order to withhold information that it is believed may lead to the recovery of the two documents mentioned in the letter, Christ power and Truth power. With these exceptions the letter is exactly reproduced, its original being in the handwriting of Lieber.[13]

When the editorial work on the Haushalter book was in progress in the early 1930's, the critical study of Francis Lieber's life by Frank Freidel had not been published. Hence, those responsible for the Haushalter study may plead extenuating circumstances for some of their mistaken judgments upon Francis Lieber based upon Thomas S. Perry's *The Life and Letters of Francis Lieber*.

By placing the verdicts on the two biographies in parallel columns, the progress in scholarship since Perry's day comes very clearly into focus. Haushalter appears in the first column, Freidel in the second:

In 1882 Thomas S. Perry published his deeply interesting book *The Life and Letters of Francis Lieber*. He says that when preparing his work, he made it his rule to "alter Lieber's phraseology as little as pos-	The standard biography of Lieber is Thomas Sergeant Perry (ed.) *The Life and Letters of Francis Lieber* (*Boston, 1881*) which is a compilation of excerpts from Lieber's letters and journals, pre-

sible, to give to the world what Lieber, who was using a foreign tongue, really wrote—not what he might have written had he learned English earlier... It is impossible not to admire his command of our language." [14]

pared under the close scrutiny of his widow. Perry...was at the time young and inexperienced. He hastily cut Matilda Lieber's compilation from two volumes to one, and in so doing excluded all mention of some phases of Lieber's career and rendered o t h e r s unintelligible. Perry made use of only a small part of the letters written by Lieber, and printed only six of those received by him. In the approved fashion of the time, Perry polished his subject's Germanisms, telescoped and garbled materials, linked together letters of several dates to form new ones, and failed to supply adequate or accurate editorial explanations. [15]

The two libraries in which many of the findings of this inquiry were verified were the Henry E. Huntington Library in San Marino, California, and the Hoose Library of the University of Southern California.

The former library has a large collection of genuine Francis Lieber materials such as papers with notes, pamphlets, and over 2,500 letters written by Lieber. Miss Norma Cuthbert, the head cataloguer in the Department of Manuscripts, not only made all these data available for examination but cooperated in many ways in guiding us to more defendable conclusions, yet must not in any respect be charged with responsibility for any of the conclusions reached. [16]

The Hoose Library, in addition to its excellent selection of general philosophical books, has lately come into possession of some of W. T. Harris's correspondence.

Freidel's conclusions regarding the documents examined in this study representing the most recent critical findings must not be omitted from this Foreword:

A manuscript ascribed to Lieber which is of considerable interest is an essay on "The Metaphysical Religion of Hegel" . . . It forms the basis for significant passages in *Science and Health*.

The present writer has examined the photostats of the manuscript at
Johns Hopkins University. In many essential ways the handwriting
seems to differ from that of Lieber. The hand of the manuscript and of
the alleged endorsement by Mary Baker Eddy bear a marked resemblance. Among the many thousands of Lieber letters examined by the
present writer not one was to or from, or mentioned Hiram Crafts.
The phrasing and concepts of the letter and essay are not characteristic
of Lieber . . . consequently the authenticity of the document seems
open to serious doubt, and it has not been used in this account of
Lieber.[17]

Numerous philosophers interested in Hegel the country over
gladly responded to my requests for verdicts upon the validity of
the interpretation of Hegel in the "Lieber" essay. To them my
gratitude is deep.

Mr. Knut Gundersen, a graduate student in History of Christianity in the School of Religion of the University of Southern
California, not only critically reviewed my conclusions but added
many new insights which enabled me to reinforce my argument
at various points.

Finally, my early historical studies induced me to accept Adolf
von Harnack's ideal that "every historical study is an *ethical* task."
In the light of the accumulation of data contradicting the allegations in the volume under scrutiny, it seemed to me to be the duty
of some American church historian, preferably one who was not
a member of the Christian Science Church, to call attention to the
actual significance of the "Lieber" documents.

Harnack's view was this:

In taking up a theological book we are in the habit of inquiring first
of all as to the point of view of the author. In an historical work there
is no room for such inquiry. The question here is, whether the author
is in sympathy with the subject about which he writes, whether he
can distinguish original elements from those that are derived, whether
he has a thorough acquaintance with his material, whether is conscious of the limits of historical knowledge, and whether he is truthful.
These requirements constitute the categorical imperative for the historian: but they can only be fulfilled by an unwearied self-discipline.
Hence, every historical study is an ethical task. The historian ought to
be faithful in every sense of the word; whether he has been so or not
is the question on which his readers have to decide.

FOREWORD

We hope the reader of *Ordeal by Concordance* will not be obliged to accuse us of too many failures to meet this high standard.

CONRAD HENRY MOEHLMAN

School of Religion, University of Southern California,
Los Angeles, California
June 3, 1955

PART I

The Mysterious Covering Letter

1

Some Literary Remains Are Purchased

IN THE early 1930s there dwelt in Avon, Massachusetts, we are told by Mr. Walter M. Haushalter, a man who for three decades had been an "elder" in the Baptist church there and was a highly respected citizen.[1]

The "elder's" name was S. Minot Crane. Born in 1846, he was then in his eighties.[2] His home was across the way from that of one Hiram Crafts. As neighbor and trusted friend, Crafts was well acquainted with Crane.

"In the early eighties" [3] Crafts stopped in one day and handed neighbor Crane a package for safekeeping. In the bundle was a letter dated April 1, 1866, and addressed to "Mr. Hiram Crafts, Secretary of Kantian Society, Boston Lyceum" and written by "Francis Lieber." The prize in the package was an essay entitled "The Metaphysical Religion of Hegel" likewise authored by the great "Francis Lieber." This essay was merely entrusted to the protecting care of Crafts, for the postscript signed again by "Lieber" definitely states: "Krause will arrange with you to send the Manuscripts to Berlin where he will try to publish them (Follen's wish too). Lieber." "Lieber" desired to have his essays published immediately, not tucked away and kept secret until 1930! [4] Indeed, according to the body of the covering letter, "Lieber" desired Crafts to "keep the Hegel papers safely for me" "until I call for them." He anticipated an early trip to Boston on government business.[5] Krause, not "Lieber," apparently is the mailman between New York and Boston for the covering letter. The essay was to be published in Berlin, not in Boston.

Are these contradictory directions the first clue that the present covering letter was not written by Francis Lieber and that its inventor had before him another invention which he was trying to integrate with the covering letter, now a preface to the essay? Is this assumption supported by all the confusion in the covering letter regarding the alleged pseudonym "Christian Herrmann"? [6]

Allegedly Crafts had kept essay and covering letter in his possession from 1866 to the early eighties instead of complying with the known desire of "Lieber" for immediate publication. Then Elder S. Minot Crane had them in his Avon, Massachusetts, home from "the early eighties" [7] for "fifty years," instead of proceeding to publication or returning the bundle to the heirs of Lieber, to whom the materials belonged. The manuscripts contain no direction to conceal these papers from the public. In the early thirties, Crane felt he could sell them to Mr. Haushalter provided they would "not be suppressed." A bill of sale was drawn up and the desire of both Crafts and Crane drew nearer realization. An affidavit secured from Crane's family describes "much of the history of the document, its transmissal and descent, and Mrs. Eddy's access to it." [9] Think of a person who has suppressed unusual materials for about half a century suddenly deciding that they just must be published when a monetary consideration enters the story!

Mr. Crane, it is said, was thinking of making "a provision in his will that would insure the document being made public *after his death*." Yet, "for fifty years" he could have rid himself of all worries by simply returning the documents to their rightful owners. How strange mortals are! "For fifty years" he felt that he had been handed "a thankless mission and a vicarious burden," [10] but it never occurred to him to solve his problem by returning the literary bundle to its legal owners. But then there would have been no continuation of the story.

It is quite important to point out that the only external indication of date of origin of the "Lieber" documents alleged is the memory of a man over eighty years old who was of the opinion that neighbor Crafts had handed them to him in the early eighties.

In discoveries by amateurs, affidavits are often furnished by the family in support of a father's or a mother's statement, and in quantity. So also in Avon on this occasion, an affidavit was secured to guarantee the authenticity of the "Lieber" materials.[11] Recall that the alleged immersion of General George Washington by a Baptist chaplain in an icebound creek at Valley Forge was supported by numerous affidavits of descendants of the officiating chaplain decades later but the chaplain's own son never breathed a word of it to anyone.

The Haushalter book does not print the affidavit but contents itself with the statement that it "describes much of the history of the Document, its transmissal and descent, and Mrs. Eddy's access to it." Well, all the more reason, then, to have published it. The affidavits regarding the immersion of General George Washington were published in full, signed before a notary public, and vouched for by him, and yet were shown to be in error.

A bill of sale and the payment of the purchase price brought the "Lieber" letter and essay and some personal papers (of Craft's) and an "announcement of a new book by Andrew Jackson Davis," a spiritualist, into the possession of the author-editor of *Mrs. Eddy Purloins from Hegel*.[12] As the reader tries to visualize the little group in the Crane home that day in 1930, all gazing at "Lieber" property, he again is amazed that, with the name "Francis Lieber" or "Lieber" signed twice to a one-page letter and appearing once on the title page of the twelve-page essay, again at the head of the essay and finally at the end of the essay, and for extra good measure as the very last signature following the last "note" on page 12 of "The Metaphysical Religion of Hegel," six times in all, leaving no doubt that the materials belonged to "Lieber" (and since his death in 1872 to his heirs), someone in the circle should not have suggested that the discovery be immediately communciated to the Lieber heirs. Did not the directive in the "Lieber" letter to Crafts read: "Keep the Hegel papers *safely for me* along with the others *until I call for them*"?[13]

If they were genuine papers of Francis Lieber, they did not belong to Crafts, and there was no directive to pass them along to neighbor Crane for safekeeping until someone might purchase them in the distant future.

As the story reads in Haushalter's book, Crafts in the early eighties had in his possession manuscripts belonging to Francis Lieber and definitely claimed by him as his property and yet he deposited these for safekeeping with friend and neighbor Crane to be kept as a secret trust instead of passing them on to their legal owners, the Lieber heirs. If these materials had been published in the early eighties, their genuineness or falsity could have been established forth-with.

In 1930, Lieber had been dead almost six decades; Follen, nine decades; W. T. Harris, over two decades. The contents of both letter and essay were cold indeed. And Crane himself was fourscore and four and for half a century had not got in touch with the legal heirs of Francis Lieber. Did not the bundle weigh heavily on his Baptist conscience?

How is this extraordinary behavior on the part of Crafts, a friend of Mrs. Eddy, and of Baptist Elder Crane to be explained? At this point one may only conjecture. Would there have been too many persons around in the 1880s to smile and sneer at the suggestion of letting the great Francis Lieber be proclaimed author of a tiny twelve-page essay on "The Metaphysical Religion of Hegel" of trivial content as far as the quotes from Hegel are concerned, with Lieber coaxing a publisher to take it? Would the actual author of the essay at that time have been compelled to meet a verbal barrage of ugly questions and charges from the Harris-Hegelians at Concord, not to mention some further queries from other authors who would have recognized materials "purloined" from their books? "The early eighties" would indeed have been a most unfortunate time to have published this bundle of "Lieber" writings.

Is the covering letter of twentieth-century date in its present form? Do its contradictions imply revision and reconstruction to fit it into the pattern of the essay? The analysis of the covering letter in the next chapter should shed some light upon these historical doubts.

2

Historical Doubts Regarding the Covering Letter

THE covering letter is dated April 1, 1866.[1] This was an Easter Sunday, but the writer does not refer to the fact. It was also April Fool's Day and may have been chosen slyly to hint at his intention to fool as many persons as possible. The year 1866 was six years before the death of Francis Lieber and nine years before the appearance of the First Edition of *Science and Health.*

One reason for choosing 1866 as the date of the letter may have been the desire to involve Hiram Crafts with the production of the essay. Crafts was converted from spiritualism to Christian Science in the late autumn of 1866. It was in 1866, too, that an early center of Hegelianism in the United States was organized at St. Louis, Missouri, by Harris, Brockmeyer, and Snider. The removal of this center to Concord, Massachusetts, increased Hegelian interest in the East in the early eighties. Other reasons that suggest themselves are Quimby's death and Mrs. Eddy's call in 1866.

Lieber's home in 1866 was in New York City at 48 East 34th Street.[2] He was then a professor in the Law School of Columbia College.[3] On April 9 he delivered two lectures on American citizenship.[4] His principal duties at this time were connected with the analysis of Confederate archives, a task to which he had been appointed in July, 1865, by the Secretary of War.[5]

This assignment was both a rush job and an arduous undertaking. It is thus described:

A total of 499 boxes and barrels of records, together with three wagon-loads of mail, were placed in Lieber's custody in August, 1865. Lieber submitted the first general report January 18, 1866. In the late

7

spring of 1866 he made reports to the House Committee of the Judiciary. On May 16, he writes to General Halleck: "I wish of course that men like you would read the report and the copies of the many letters I sent along with it. Some 270,000 . . . letters have been examined for this and other purposes. There remain I dare say some 6000 to be examined and to be briefed.[6]

Under the pressure of this work, Lieber's correspondence decreased and his social life was temporarily disrupted. Since Washington, D.C., was the center of this activity and since, in the spring of 1866, Lieber was going back and forth between New York and the capital usually by night train, it is difficult to understand how he could have found the time to write on Hegel and take a boat trip to Boston.

Indeed, on March 20 Lieber was in New York, whither he had but recently returned from Washington. On March 21 he wrote to Sumner and on March 23 he wrote to Sumner and Halleck from New York. On Palm Sunday, March 25, Lieber wrote to his friend Sumner: "This week I go again to Washington"—implying a stay of some days there.[7] He may have employed the short recess of Congress to catch up on his archives work. There is no letter in the Lieber Collection dated April 1 and no evidence of any dependable kind that he was aboard a Boston-bound boat.

On April 4, Lieber wrote on "American Citizenship" at New York.[8] On April 5 he wrote to Martin R. Thayer from New York and answered some questionnaires there. On April 9 Lieber wrote to Sumner from New York that he had delivered two lectures in the Law School of Columbia College.

All this seems to put Lieber in New York on both April 1 and April 7. The covering letter does not claim he was on a boat to Boston on either day; *this is merely inserted commentary by the editor.* Indeed, a Boston trip on either day is out of the question since Lieber was in New York City on both April 4 and April 9. The jet plane is a later invention.

No place of origin of the covering letter is given. This may imply a desire on the writer's part to protect himself against detection. It also indicates unfamiliarity with Lieber's usual letter style. Lieber usually accompanied his date with the name of the town in which he was at the time.

The covering letter begins: "Mr. Hiram Crafts, Secretary of

8

Kantian Society, Boston Lyceum." When Francis Lieber now and then mentioned the full name and address of the addressee, it was at the *end of the letter and not preceding the salutation as in this mysterious covering letter*. Out of fifty-six letters written by Lieber between January 3 and October 25, 1866, eleven have name and address at the end. Not one has name and address before the salutation.

In these letters the salutation is occasionally omitted. Otherwise, combinations such as my dear or dear (surname, title, sir, or friend) appear in general correspondence. Out of some 2,550 letters written by Lieber in the Huntington Library Collection not one begins with "Friend So-and-so" as in the covering letter.[9] Never does Lieber employ given names alone in his salutation as is the case in this covering letter.[10]

The covering letter ends with, "Truly, Francis Lieber, 'Christian Herrmann.'" In the above-mentioned fifty-six letters, not one has this single word as closing greeting. We find such words and phrases as "your(s)," "(very) truly," "very truly your(s)," "ever your(s)," "your friend and servant," "your warm-knit friend." Of these various usages, Lieber most often wrote "Ever your(s)."

Lieber often scribbled some hasty notes at the end of a letter. Usually he wrote no separate heading, but occasionally he would write "P.S." There is no instance of "Post" or "Note" as appears in the "Lieber" manuscript and the accompanying letter.

Twenty-one of the fifty-six letters mentioned above have additional remarks. Six of these remarks are signed "F.L." The others have no signature beyond the one in the main letter. Elsewhere in the Lieber correspondence the full signature does occur under an additional note. But the signature "Lieber" alone, under an added note as the covering letter manuscript has it, does not occur.

The "Lieber" manuscript has a style different from that of Lieber. Lieber was more independent and relied less upon quotations than did the author of the manuscript.

Moreover, the "Lieber" manuscript and the covering letter were written by one who differentiates between himself and any American.[11] The inventor doubtless assumed this was a trait of the historical Lieber's. But Francis Lieber soon acquired American citizenship.[12] He was proud of his adopted country; even though he remained emotionally attached to his native Germany, he could write "we Americans," "our America," and "the Germans," [13] quite contrary to the spirit of the "Lieber" of the manuscript and the accompanying letter.

Francis Lieber on March 23, 1866, just a week prior to the alleged date of the covering letter *and the copying of essay*, wrote to his friend General Halleck: "In former times I would have sat down with Mrs. Lieber and translated the article for the *United States Service Magazine, but I disrelish such things now.*"

The covering letter begins "As I said in my last letter to you," implying something like regular correspondence with Crafts. But one who has critically examined many thousand letters in the Lieber correspondence was not able to find the name of Hiram Crafts mentioned even once.[14]

There are three lists of correspondents with Francis Lieber in the Lieber Collection: (1) Letters of Introduction, (2) General List of Correspondents, (3) List of Correspondents and Dates of their Letters. The first list contains mostly letters to and from prominent persons; the second list, also handwritten, has the names of over 250 correspondents to 1872, the year of Lieber's death; the third list has some 150 correspondents between 1842 and 1848 in addition to a large number of names chronologically arranged from 1830 to 1872. *In none of these lists does the name of Hiram Crafts appear.*

Hiram Crafts confesses that he was taught Christian Science by Mrs. Eddy in 1866:

> At that time I was a Spiritualist, *but her teachings changed my views on that subject and I gave up Spiritualism.* She never taught me in my mental practice to hurt others but only to heal the sick and *reform the sinner. She taught me from the Scriptures and from manuscripts that she wrote as she taught me.*[15]

In the spring of 1866, the date of the covering letter, Hiram S. Crafts was a spiritualist, not a secretary of a mythical Kantian Society in Boston Lyceum. He was probably returning from his winter factory job in Lynn to his summer cobbling job in Stoughton. In the fall of 1866 Crafts was a student of Mrs. Eddy's, who was tutoring him in the "new Science of religion" on the basis of the Scriptures and her original manuscripts and not his teacher on the basis of the then-nonexistent "Metaphysical Religion of Hegel."

Hiram S. Crafts was not a resident of Boston in 1866 but of

Stoughton (now Avon) some sixteen miles south of Boston. In the autumn of that year, Mrs. Eddy was boarding at the home of George D. Clark of Lynn. In search of employment during the winter in one of the shoe factories of Lynn, Crafts journeyed there with his wife and while there boarded at the Clarks'. Here he met Mrs. Eddy and listened to her arguments against "Rochester, New York, rapping-Spiritualism." He abandoned spiritualism and turned not to Hegelianism but to religious healing, or Mind-science, under the tutoring of Mrs. Eddy.

Just how Francis Lieber, only thirty-two years of age when he left Boston in 1832, could have become acquainted with one Hiram Crafts, not living there and scarcely out of shorts, is another of the innumerable mysteries connected with the literary bundle Crafts allegedly deposited with S. Minot Crane.

The letter is addressed to "Mr. Hiram Crafts, Secretary of Kantian Society, Boston Lyceum." There was no such society in Boston.[16] There had been a "Free Religious Club" (later called "Boston Radical Club") in Boston of which Mrs. Julia Ward Howe had been a member. Its regular program, on the first Monday of each month, consisted of the reading of a paper and its discussion. In her *Reminiscences*, Mrs. Howe writes: "I did indeed hear at these meetings much that pained and even irritated me. The disposition to seek outside the limits of Christianity for all that is noble and inspiring in religious culture..."[17] There had been a Kantian Society in St. Louis from 1877 to 1879 and at intervals to 1887.[18] It may be that knowledge of these facts suggested to the twentieth-century inventor of the covering letter the perpetration of this astounding blunder of a Boston Kantian Society, assured that the gullible reader would not raise any question as to its authenticity. A list of even a few of the literary inventions accepted "on faith" by Americans and Europeans alike in the nineteenth and twentieth centuries[19] should result in general approval of our explanation.[20]

The covering letter next claims that "Lieber" is the author of three Hegelian papers: the "Essay," "Christ Power," and "Truth Power." The Essay will be studied in a later section.

Before 1936, when the hypothesis under review was published, Francis Lieber was known as a political scientist and a man of culture who naturally would have in his personal library German books on philosophy and religion. Friedrich Strauss' *Leben Jesu*, for example, was in the library of numerous ministers totally unaware of the historical importance of that treatise. Francis Lieber's area of research was history, political economy, penal law, political ethics, legal and political hermeneutics, property and labor, civil liberty, international law and copyright, a code for the government of armies. His correspondence was largely with men of prominence in the political and legal realm, with congressmen, European historians and statesmen, generals, presidents, members of the Supreme Court of the United States, and law-enforcement officers.

"Lieber" continues: "The Hegel papers are my best. All three grew out of my conversations with my old and very dear friend, Charles Follen, who attended the first meetings thirty years ago." Thirty subtracted from 1865, when the essay was written, equals 1835. Lieber was then either in Philadelphia or in Columbia, South Carolina.

The Charles Follen was presumably K. T. C. Follen, born in 1796 in Germany, a lecturer at the University of Jena twenty-two years later, and a leader of the revolutionary *Burschenschaften*. In 1820 he escaped to Switzerland, going on to Paris and to Basel, finally landing in New York in 1824. Harvard appointed him instructor in gymnastics in the following year and later ethics and history were added to his curricular activity. At the age of thirty-four, Follen became professor of German at Harvard for a term of five years. Acquiring American citizenship, he both joined and aided the activities of the New England abolitionist movement. Upon the expiration of his term as professor of German at Cambridge, Follen supported himself by tutoring, lecturing, and preaching.

He was a friend of various New England religious and social leaders, including the great Channing. On January 3, 1840, at the age of forty-four, he was aboard the ill-fated steamer *Lexington*, which sank in Long Island Sound. He had been married to Eliza Lee Cabot for a dozen years. His brilliant wife published a five-volume study of his life and writings.

This Charles Follen had been a very close friend of Lieber's and had been instrumental in bringing Lieber to America.[21] The friendship seems to have been based on practical need, rather than on philosophical considerations. In his youth Follen had been a leader of the *Burschenschaft* and had apparently been associated with Jahn and his *Turner* movement.[22] Lieber, who fell under suspicion for

12

being associated with the group around Follen and the political assassinator Karl Sand, may not have been a member of the Follen group at all. Bruncken, who studied the environmental background of Lieber in Germany, comes to the following conclusion:

The leading spirit of this group was Karl Follenius (Charles Follen), who afterwards became a Unitarian minister in New England. We have no evidence that Lieber had any connection with these amateur conspirators, nor do we even know that he ever belonged to the *"Burschenschaft."* [23]

A note in Lieber's diary, four years after reaching the United States (1831), reads:

May 24. In the evening, before going to bed, I took up by chance the songs which Jahn wrote for the celebration of the 18th of October. They made me very sad. That an enthusiasm so hollow, so unhealthy and unnatural, could exist to such an extent amongst those who seemed to be the most ready to do something for the people, is painful.

The friendship between Follen and Lieber seems to have decreased as their similar experiences in Germany came to mean less and less to Lieber. The year after the above diary quotation Lieber became an American citizen.[24] Two years later he published a book that was in direct competition to one already written by Follen.[25]

A recent interpretation of Follen was written by René Weller and indicates how absurdly dull it was for the covering letter to make Follen the founder of a nonexistent "Kantian Society, Boston Lyceum." Our inventor should have selected some really prominent Kantian as one of his authorities. His remarks upon Follen seriously reduce the authenticity of the covering letter. To substantiate the point consider these excerpts from Weller:

In the course of a brief history of ethics which discusses the Greeks, the New Testament, and Spinoza, we get a fairly full exposition of Kant's philosophy. The description of the *Critique of Pure Reason* is elementary and vitiated by Follen's repeated reference to time, space, and categories as "innate ideas": he suspects Kant's system of leading to subjective idealism and skepticism, but then gives an exposition of the moral philosophy which shows far better insight and even critical acumen. Kant is criticized for his mistakes of considering man "sometimes entirely as a rational and moral, and sometimes entirely as a sensual or phenomenal being," and some good points are scored against the categorical imperative, which to Follen appears vague and general and merely an advice to search the nature, particularly the rational and moral nature, of man. Kant's religion of reason seems to him "nothing less than an avowal of atheism." *His attitude toward Kant is extremely unsympathetic: he criticizes him not from the point of view of later German idealism (which he apparently did not know though he alludes to Fichte)*, but with empirical arguments which he manages to combine with a philosophy of faith...Though Follen, in spite of his premature death, did something to foster interest in things German, he can scarcely be described as a propagandist for German idealist philosophy.[26]

An oft-quoted American philosopher has written: Follen "knew little philosophy and had little sympathy for the post-Kantians" of whom Hegel was one.[27]

Read this paper under the pen-name Follen gave me "Christian Herrmann." I do not want my Professor title involved in religious controversy. Follen got a lesson there. The publishers told him they did not want to help German atheism, so uninformed are they here yet. But a few years Hiram and you shall see the triumph of German metaphysics all over the world.[28]

Since "Lieber" signs his name "Francis Lieber" and "Lieber" in the covering letter; "Francis Lieber" on the title page of the essay on "The Metaphysical Religion of Hegel"; once on page 1; once on page 12; and "Lieber" on page 12, it is difficult to understand what protection his pseudonym afforded. Moreover, he had been transferred from a professorship at Columbia University in New York in 1865 to the Law School there in a controversy, and ten years earlier from a professorship in Columbia, South Carolina. The historical Lieber could not have written this sentence.

The inventor of this covering letter did know that Francis Lieber employed pen names occasionally [29] and cleverly put the fact to good use in the covering letter. Francis Lieber also wrote *inter nos* letters and insisted upon anonymity in his articles, pamphlets, and letters.[30]

But search has not produced a Francis Lieber letter or article which first signs his actual name and then adds a pen name: "Truly Francis Lieber 'Christian Herrmann' "; "The Metaphysical Religion of Hegel. Francis Lieber, 'Christian Herrmann,' April, 1866"; "Francis Lieber 'Christian Herrmann' "; "Lieber"; "The Metaphysical

Religion of Hegel by Francis Lieber—Christian Herrmann; Lieber."
The actual name of Lieber appears six times in the fourteen pages
and the pen name with it four times. The pen name never appears in
postscript or notes! There was no theoretical or practical significance for the use of the pen name in this situation as if to say: "My
real name is Francis Lieber, but I wish you to conceal it by calling
me 'Christian Herrmann' "! Such a publicity stunt was unworthy of
Francis Lieber. Does it not rather indicate the prior existence of a
letter by "Christian Herrmann," a fictitious character, as the actual
writer of a letter which when modified for use in the alleged "Lieber" essay could survive only as a ghost, namely, as the pen name
for the alleged author of that essay, Francis Lieber? Was the covering letter purchased around 1930 really the original covering letter
in the bundle handed S. Minot Crane "in the early eighties"? Had
the contents of that bundle been added to?

"But a few years Hiram and you shall see the triumph of German
metaphysics all over the world"! This apocalyptic prophecy fits a
later time ever so much better than April, 1866.

"Tell the Society I would like to meet them again. I plead with
them to shun spiritualism; it is full of deadly evils. Cultivate the German philosophy—Kant and Hegel—as our founder Follen said."

"Francis Lieber," who had never attended a meeting of the Boston Kantian Society which had never met, would like to meet the
ghosts again:

The second mystery here is: "shun spiritualism."

Why is "shun spiritualism" associated with "cultivate . . . Kant
and Hegel"? Because the inventor knew that in Germany "spiritualism" denoted the idealistic philosophy and he did not mean that kind
of "spiritualism" but the "Rochester rapping" kind that Mrs. Eddy
had opposed.

The sermonette against spiritualism may also have been introduced
to make the addressee of the covering letter more lifelike. For Hiram
Crafts was converted from faith in it by Mrs. Eddy in the late
autumn of 1866.[31] Crafts is described as "possessing an ordinary
intelligence, a common school education, and a tendency toward
transcendentalism," which he had absorbed from the discussions
going on in Emersonian and Parkerian circles.[32]

What Crafts knew about Christian Science he had learned from
Mrs. Eddy. She had instructed him from the Bible and her own

writings. Two decades after "the early eighties" Crafts was still true to her teachings as far as he comprehended them. With a knowledge of all this in his possession through the various biographies of Mrs. Eddy, the inventor of the Hegel essay was increasing faith in its authenticity by these historical touches.

In the bundle of 1930, one recalls, in addition to the "Lieber" materials, there was discovered "a printed announcement of a new book by Andrew Jackson Davis," described by Haushalter as a Swedenborgian.[33] The inventor seems thus to be suggesting slyly that Crafts was still interested in spiritualism in later life in spite of his conversion from it in 1866.

"This letter and the Hegel document come to you by our common friend . . ."

This is the first instance of an erasure or blocking out in the facsimile by the editor-author: There are six other such omissions in this brief covering letter. The apology for such extraordinary procedure was explained thus:

In both the photographic and printed reproduction of the letter Dr. Lieber sent to Crafts along with the paper he had laboriously prepared to be read before the Kantian Society, blanks appear where certain names have been omitted. The omission has been made in order to withhold information that it is believed may lead to the recovery of the two documents mentioned in the letter, *Christ power* and *Truth power*. With these exceptions the letter is exactly reproduced, its original being in the handwriting of Lieber. As a human document the letter is soul revealing.[34]

The "common friend" was Otto Krause, as examination of the photostat at Princeton Theological Seminary Library showed. So now we know at last assuredly that "Otto Krause" was the alleged mail carrier in the mind of the inventor. He, not "Lieber," carried the covering letter and "The Metaphysical Religion of Hegel" to "Mr. Hiram Crafts" in "Boston." "Lieber" says so twice: "This letter and the Hegel document come to you by our common friend Otto Krause"; "Krause will arrange with you to send the manuscripts to Berlin . . ."

And since both the covering letter and the essay were in Otto's satchel, just how could the ubiquitous "Lieber" be writing the letter aboard that "New York to Boston boat," not to mention his giving the letter and essay to fictitious Crafts of the Kantian Society, Boston Lyceum! Our inventor is very, very confused.

No Otto Krause appears in the index of Freidel's biography of Lieber. The name of Albert(?) Krause mentioned in the essay [35] may have suggested the use of the name "Otto Krause" as well as his vocation as student of philosophy, naturally at Berlin. It was natural, too, to pass on Otto to "Lieber's" Berlin relatives. In return for all "Lieber's" kindness, Otto would try to sell the great man's twelve-page essay on Hegel in the capital of Prussia, the city that contained so many articles and books on Hegel and by Hegel as to make the twelve-page "Lieber" adventure into error the talk of the town for months without end! [36] The humor of the covering letter here reaches its climax! To seek a publisher for a twelve-page essay on Hegel in English by an American in the Berlin of 1866 must have been regarded as the boner of the century! This was bringing oil to Texas.

The covering letter next addresses itself to Otto Krause's trip to Berlin and Munich and his quarrel with his girl friend, Louise. The pertinence of this to the meeting of the alleged Kantian Society in Boston is not obvious. The ship-sailing references are very interesting and assume that "Lieber" has done some research in this area also.

Otto desired to sail direct from New York to Germany on the *Bremen*, but found the fare too high. So he is arranging to go to Boston and sail from there on the *Asia* of the Royal Mail if he can get a chance to earn his passage. "By second, it is sixty dollars, but he can scarce afford even that."

This *Bremen* had been built in 1858, was in the service of the North German Lloyd, had a tonnage of 11,570, measured 550 feet by 60 feet, had twin screws, 2 masts and 2 funnels, and made 15.5 knots an hour. It carried United States mail. The passage from New York to Bremen first cabin was $105.00, and second cabin $62.50, steerage $37.50, and it sailed from New York on April 26.

But Otto Krause, the letter tells us, was a poor man, he could not pay his passage on the *Bremen*. He was also a very simple man, and could not add well. For he decided instead of going from New York to Bremen for $37.50, to pay the fare from New York to Boston, and there take the *Asia* of the Cunard Line stopping at Halifax and at Queenstown and arriving at Liverpool whence Otto would have to pay additional fare to get to Munich.

This *Asia* was commissioned in 1850, had a tonnage of only 2,227, measured 268 feet by 45 feet, consumed 76 tons of coal a day, was a paddle-wheeler, with 3 masts and one funnel, made only 12 knots an hour, made its last sailing for the Cunard Company in 1867, next year was sold and converted into a sailing ship and in 1878 was destroyed by fire at Bombay, India.

First-cabin passage on the *Asia*, Boston to Liverpool, was $112.50; second cabin, $65.00. Add the New York to Boston fare and the Liverpool to Munich fare, and poor Otto would have been considerably in the red, not to mention the additional time plus meals and lodging expenses. One wonders whether Otto ever picked up the small inheritance awaiting him at Munich or continued his philosophical studies at Berlin or ever existed except in the imagination of the inventor. How Lieber, living in New York and busy with government affairs involving the settlement of Confederate archive problems, knew so much about Boston boats is another unsolved mystery.[37] Apocalyptic "Lieber" should have been appointed the first professor of comprehensive knowledge in the United States!

The next paragraph in the covering letter makes Crafts an intimate friend of Otto and Louise, who have become estranged. Otto is going to Munich to collect a small inheritance but will not linger there long, since Munich is Catholic and "intollerant" and Berlin offers better opportunities to study philosophy. Be sure to write him about Louise.

The next to the last paragraph fascinates one as an indication of editorial incompetency. Since the covering letter is a fabrication, it is stupid to wonder about its place of origin so far as Francis Lieber is concerned. One thing is certain. It was not written aboard a "New York to Boston boat," since then no letter would have been called for. Lieber would have handed the document to Crafts in person. Indeed, he might have read it himself to the meeting of the ghostly-Bostonian-Kantians. But the New York to Boston boat absurdity cannot fairly be blamed upon the jokester who wrote the covering letter.

This paragraph reads: "Long hours have been spent in copying this manuscript all done under the difficulties of this old ship [New York-Boston boat]. Keep the Hegel papers safely for me along with the others until I call for them. Govt. business may bring me to Boston soon."

Obviously "Lieber" was not on the New York to Boston boat!
Turning to the facsimile we find no claim that he was. The words
within the brackets were inserted by the editor-author of the Haushalter volume. This is one of several blunders regarding German
usage appearing in this book. A German colloquialism for the infir-
mities of old age—rheumatism, arthritis, ulcers, false teeth, dim
eyes, ears that are closed, when the sound of the mill is low, and one
rises at the twittering of the birds, when the daughters of song lie
prostrate, when one ascends the steps out of breath, and the hair
grows gray and the silver cord is snapped and the brain broken and
whatever else may be found in Ecclesiastes 12—is "this old ship."
The ghost-author employed this German colloquialism to confuse
any future reader of the covering letter. Apparently he was very
successful in the case of the editor-author. Really in 1866 the genuine Francis Lieber was hard at work collecting and assorting and
interpreting the tons of material the Union forces had "acquired"
from the Confederacy. The letter definitely states that Otto Krause
was carrying a letter and document, given him by "Lieber," to
Boston.

"My friendship to the Kantian Brothers and Friends"—there was
no Kantian Society, Boston Lyceum. The year 1866 is too early for
Concord and even for St. Louis Hegelianism.

> Truly
> > Francis Lieber
> > > "Christian Herrmann"

Post: *Krause* will arrange with you to send the Manuscripts to *Berlin*
where he will try to publish them (Follen's wish too).

> > > > Lieber.

Follen perished in a sea disaster in 1840. Lieber and Follen had
drifted apart in the early thirties. Would Lieber in 1865 have pro-
ceeded according to a suggestion of the long, long ago? Why would
Follen have been interested, thirty years before the essay appeared,
in the precise place of publication?

Our story of "The Metaphysical Religion of Hegel" will demonstrate conclusively how fantastic this covering letter really is.

3

Francis Lieber and the Covering Letter

COULD the Lieber of history have composed the covering letter? After the year 1835, Lieber's life was devoted to political science. To summarize what Lieber accomplished in this field we quote a few estimates out of scores available.

R. G. Gettell, in his *History of Political Thought*, pointed out that Schelling held that "the state was a natural organism, representing a phase of the historical world process." Hegel went on from there to interpret the state as a real person with the individual existing for it and the monarch as the personification of the state, agreements between states were provisional, war was inevitable and not altogether undesirable, the state was an end in itself and its evolution had been from the Oriental state with only the despot free to the German state with all free.

"Francis Lieber," while holding to a "modified natural law philosophy, introduced the organic and evolutionary conception of the state and laid emphasis on the growth of a national spirit." [1]

T. V. Parrington, in his *Main Currents in American Thought*, interprets Francis Lieber's political philosophy as undermining the compact theory of government and the natural rights philosophy and substituting for them the idea of a sovereign political authority which finally interpreted the order of life for its subjects, transforming the citizen into subject and granting the state unlimited power over its subjects. But this nationalism was to be government by law and the historically developed institutions, customs, mores. His two fatal errors were his legalism and the divorce between politics and economics so that his influence in general has been against the liberty he hoped for. [2]

20

Herbert W. Schneider lets Francis Lieber deny the "divine right of the people" and states that his one claim to fame was that he described "institutional government as the political embodiment of self-reliance and mutual acknowledgement of self-rule. It is in this view the political realization of equality." [3]

The author and collaborators of *Mrs. Eddy Purloins from Hegel* have discovered a new "Francis Lieber" very dissimilar to the Francis Lieber of history—a Lieber of myth, of faith, who wrote an essay upon "The Metaphysical Religion of Hegel" and in a covering letter directed that a pen name be substituted for his own when he was sixty-six years of age and had achieved an extraordinary reputation for courage in the American period of his career. The Lieber of history wrote, a year before his death: "Yes, my dear Sir, I fought at Waterloo and was afterwards expatriated because I was enthusiastic for the same ideas which Wilhelm (1871) now symbolizes and represents on his entrance into Berlin." Lieber fought against Know-Nothingism in the United States. He called Garibaldi *Justus et probus*. He favored a six-year term for the president of the United States. He proposed the slogan: "No Right without a Duty; no Duty without its Right." And he did not fear not to attend church in the South, "for all the sermons I could hear would be either fiery like Chinese dragons or drowsy like stuffed serpents." "For my soul, Christ's religion centers most in that sublimest and purest of all that exists in words—the sermon on the mount." Yet this man is accused of the incredible folly and contradiction of asking that his name in an essay to a nonexistent "Kantian Society" be withheld and "Christian Herrmann" be substituted for it while in the next second signing himself "Francis Lieber"—believe it or not!

The "Lieber" of the covering letter is boasting his authorship of "The Metaphysical Religion of Hegel"—"the Hegel papers are my best." But when the Lieber of history refers to Hegel, it is not in terms of endearment or flattery. Lieber describes Hegel as "a garrulous German professor who regarded himself as half national hero half moral scientist," [4] and "Hegel has done infinite harm to the cause of science. Instead of earnest thoughtful investigation and a discreet acknowledgement of previous experience, he is full of arrogance and presumption." [5] And in a letter to Professor Bluntschli, Lieber says: "I consider Hegel's 'spirit of history' as an independent, separate entity to be nonsense." [6]

There is in existence an essay on Hegel at least in part by Francis Lieber. It appears in the first edition of the *Encyclopedia Americana*, of which Lieber was the editor and also in some sense the author or translator. Assisted by E. Wigglesworth, Francis Lieber had prepared this edition on the basis of the seventh edition of the German *Conversations-Lexicon*.

The comment on Hegel is quoted in full:

George William Frederic Hegel, ordinary professor of philosophy at Berlin, was born at Stuttgart, August 27, 1770. His father was secretary to the ducal chamber, and provided carefully for his education. Intimate with the classical writers of ancient and modern literature, as well as with the (so-called) philosophical views on religious dogmas, he entered the university of Tübingen in his 18th year, where he devoted five years, in the theological foundation, to philosophical and theological studies. He attended particularly to the philosophical lectures; but in metaphysics, as it was then taught, did not find a satisfactory explanation of our inward operations. This impelled him to study the writings of Kant. In connection with philosophy, he also applied himself zealously to the natural sciences, as well as to mathematics and physics. To obtain a knowledge of the world, which began to be agitated with mighty convulsions, he went as a private teacher to Switzerland, and thence to Frankfort on the Main, &c. Some property, which fell to him at the death of his father enabled him to go to Jena to pursue the idea of philosophy, which he had formed. He wrote there *Ueber die Differenz der Fichte' schen und Schelling' schen Philosophie*—On the Difference between the Philosophy of Fichte and Schelling (Jena, 1801)—and published, with Schelling, the *Kritische Journal der Philosophie*—The Critical Journal of Philosophy (Jena, 1802). He also began to deliver lectures as a private teacher, and was appointed, in 1806, professor extraordinary of philosophy. At this time he was employed in preparing a work to exhibit his peculiar views in philosophy. It appeared as a *System der Wissenschaft*—System of Science (1st vol., Bamberg, 1807). In the night before the battle of Jena, he finished the last pages of the manuscript. After this catastrophe, he went to Bamberg, where he remained till he was appointed, in the autumn of 1808, by the Bavarian government, rector of the gymnasium of Nuremberg, and professor of certain branches of philosophical science. While he held this station, he completed the *Wissenschaft der Logik*—Science of Logic—which forms the first part and foundation of his philosophical system. The first part appeared in 1812, the third and last in 1816. In the Autumn of the latter year, he was invited to Heidelberg, as professor of philosophy.

Here he wrote his *Encyklopaedie der Philosophischen Wissenschaften*
—Encyclopedia of the Philosophical Sciences (Heidelberg, 2d ed., 1827)
—intended to give the public, and especially his hearers, a short view
of his course and method in philosophy. From Heidelberg, he was
invited to Berlin, in Fichte's stead, and entered upon his office in the
autumn of 1818. Here he has published his *Grundlinien des Rechts oder
Naturrechts und Staatswissenschaft in Grundrisse*—Elements of Right,
or the Basis of Natural Law and Political Science (Berlin, 1821).[7]

As an estimate of Hegel's system of philosophy, this essay is less
than superficial. It does not display any insight into the greatness of
the mind that was to suggest so many of its leading concepts to the
nineteenth century. It has one thing in common with the alleged
essay on "The Metaphysical Religion of Hegel" printed in 1936, a
century later: neither shows much knowledge of Hegel. Although
published in 1834, the article fails to mention the death of Hegel in
1831. Lieber was not sufficiently interested in Hegel to go beyond
his source for a bit of color. Freidel's judgment was that his essays
"on Goethe and Kant were able; that on Hegel worthless." [8]

In his *A History of American Philosophy*, published in 1946,
Herbert W. Schneider devotes some pages to Lieber and to Hegel.[9]
His bibliography on Lieber cites publications to 1941, yet there is
no mention of "Lieber's" "Metaphysical Religion of Hegel." [10]
Lieber, indeed, is granted only "a smathering [knowledge] of
Niebuhr's world history and of idealistic philosophy." [11]

To point up the difference in attitude between the Lieber of history and the "Lieber" of the covering letter and the essay in regard
to German idealism and metaphysics, observe that in his encyclopedia he fails to mention any German representatives or schools
when mentioning Greek, Scholastic, English, and French schools
of metaphysics, giving only a few lines to idealism and about a page
to metaphysics.

Lieber's interest was practical. *The Encyclopedia* has two pages
on Plato, one on Hegel, but eleven pages on *Canals in Great Britain*
and twenty-four pages on *Constitution*. His confession in the *Commonplace Book* (1851) is precise:

All truly great philosophy is not only a reflex and concentration or
abstraction of the state of knowledge at the time, but like all things
great, it is production of vast and great, that is substantial and comprehensive actions and movements. This is a test. What searching influence

has Kant not had on after ages. Where is the productive influence of Fichte? For, I speak only of productive effects...

So Shakespeare was superior to Socrates, Plato, Aristotle, and the rest of the Greek philosophers. "The greatest in their line are only the highest peaks of a gradually rising Alpine Chain; *but Shakespeare is a Mount Blanc* ..." This was the historical Lieber's response to a toast in the very month the "Lieber" of the essay is credited with writing it! [12]

The "Lieber" essay is superlative in its adoration of Hegel: His demonstration of immortality "places Hegel in the forefront of the world of thinkers of all times"; this is the "great Hegel, the flower of German metaphysics"; "If they had gone further they would have found a greater than Kant ... The greatest of these and the greatest of all metaphysicians is Hegel"; "Hegel is the Copernicus for the new German metaphysics of religion"; "Kant and Fichte are the ascending slope to Hegel"; "Menzel says Hegel gave himself out for God ... He even charges that Hegel's followers compared him to Christ. How unjust this is to Hegel is clear to anyone who reads his words, and especially to all who knew his humble, generous, and Christly spirit while on earth."

This is the "Lieber" of the covering letter and of the essay but not in any respect the Francis Lieber of American history.[13]

Already the reader discerns mystery written over the "Lieber" documents and when the "Francis Lieber-Christian Herrmann" hybrid signature is added, it almost makes it necessary to assume that Baptist Elder S. Minot Crane was at least hazy in his memory of what transpired "about 1883" between him and Hiram S. Crafts. Did Crane ever affirm that the author of the "Lieber" bundle was Francis Lieber? May he not have said "Christian Herrmann," who had lived in Boston? Had a real "Christian Herrmann" of Boston in an old man's memory somehow become confused with that of "Francis Lieber," who had also lived in Boston way back there?

Our conclusion thus far must be that Francis Lieber's connection with the "Lieber" documents is exceedingly doubtful and that the covering letter has been altered from its original form.[14]

4

The Handwriting of the Covering Letter and That of Francis Lieber

THE Christian Science Board of Directors regarded the allegations against its founder which appeared in the Haushalter volume as so unsubstantiated that it contented itself with this refutation:

"In 1930-1933, The Mother Church was invited to buy what was offered as proof that Mary Baker Eddy got some two hundred lines for 'Science and Health with Key to the Scriptures' (which contains eighteen thousand lines) from an admirer of Hegel's philosophy. The alleged proof consisted of two handwritten papers: (1) a purported article or essay headed 'The Metaphysical Religion of Hegel *by Christian Herrmann*'; (2) a purported letter dated April 1866 addressed to 'Friend Hiram' *and signed 'Christian Herrmann.'* The letter purported to be from a man of German birth, hard pressed for money, who was returning to Germany after a long stay in the United States. 'Friend Hiram' was said to be Mrs. Eddy's first pupil, Hiram S. Crafts.

"Not at all convinced by the papers in question, the Directors of The Mother Church declined to consider buying them.

"In 1936, there was published in Great Britain and in the United States a book by an author who participated in the foregoing attempts to sell. It included the following features, described as 'newly discovered': (1) a purported article or essay headed 'The Metaphysical Religion of Hegel *by Francis Lieber—"Christian Herrmann"*'; (2) a purported notation on the cover of the same paper, as follows: '*N.B. This is Metaphysical Basis of Healing and Science of Health* Same as "Christ-power" and "Truth-power" Mary

25

Baker'; (3) a purported letter dated April 7, 1866, addressed 'Mr. Hiram Crafts Secretary of Kantian Society Boston Lyceum. Friend Hiram' and signed 'Francis Lieber Christian Herrmann.' The book included what were represented as exact reproductions of the foregoing features in type and in handwriting. The author also asserted that the first and third of the foregoing features were written by 'none other than the noted publicist and educator, Dr. Francis Lieber.' . . .

"In 1930-1933, during the solicitations just described, none of the solicitors who spoke or wrote at that time made any assertion or claim corresponding to the purported notation by 'Mary Baker' just quoted. Nor did any of them make any assertion or claim that the letter or manuscript then offered for sale was written by Francis Lieber. On the contrary, they spoke as if Christian Herrmann were an actual person.

"After the book in question was published, The Christian Science Board of Directors, disbelieving that the documents in question were genuine and desiring opinions from disinterested experts, put specimens of Mrs. Eddy's handwriting and specimens of Francis Lieber's handwriting (of which there are plenty), with copies of the book in question, into the hands of Mr. Albert S. Osborn and Mr. Elbridge Walter Stein of New York City, who are two of the best-known authorities on handwriting and questioned documents in the United States. These experts were consulted separately, and each of them tested the documents in question separately, but both of them reported the same conclusions, and each of them reported his conclusions and his reasons for them in detail, in length, and in positive words. The gist of their findings was that neither the purported notation by Mary Baker nor the purported signature was in the handwriting of Mary Baker Eddy, and that neither the purported letter nor the purported manuscript reproduced in the book nor the purported signature of Francis Lieber was in his handwriting." [1]

Such a conclusion reversed the main contention of the Haushalter volume that Mrs. Eddy had been a plagiarist of translations of Hegel's writings even if only to a slight extent and naturally reduced the monetary value of the "Lieber" documents to next to nothing.

The accusation of plagiarism as discussed in the volume indicates such slight acquaintance with what is involved when religious dependence is the basis of the charge that serious clarification and definition of the issues are required before the internal evidence to show the utter folly of connecting Francis Lieber with these writings may be presented.

The matter of so-called "plagiarism" in case of religious literature has been much overworked by religious orthodoxy. If consistently applied to almost any sermon, there would be many red faces in the pulpits Sunday after Sunday. The sale of "preaching helps" is heavy, and even today one may hear sermons preached by Theodore Parker and Phillips Brooks long, long ago.

Take this illustration from the Haushalter volume, for example. "In ancient Rome *a plagiarius was a kidnapper, a thief of slaves or children.*" [2] Turning to the *Encyclopaedia Britannica* to verify the assertion, one is surprised to read: "The Latin *plagiarius* meant *a kidnapper*, a stealer or abductor of *a slave or a child* . . .[3] Out of sixteen words six are identical with the statement in the *Britannica* and for the adaptations "thief" for "stealer" and "in ancient Rome" for "the Latin" and "meant" for "was," the source is clear. Evidently the author had read the encyclopedia. It was the basis of his statement. Is this an instance of innocent "borrowing" or of "theft"? There does not appear to be any additional item of information in the author's definition of *plagiarius* as compared with the definition in *Britannica.*

What, then, is plagiarism?

If a society, fellowship, brotherhood meets regularly for discussion of social problems and one of the group later writes a best seller summarizing the debates with such accuracy that each member says "Why, I said that"—is the author a plagiarist? When a modern writer dresses up an ancient story and publishes a play whose sources can be traced, should he be accused of plagiarism? Are preachers whose sermons were put together from this and that book plagiarists? Was the Declaration of Independence plagiarized by Thomas Jefferson? Pickering and Adams showed that the Declaration of Independence "contained no new ideas, that it is a commonplace compilation, its sentiments hacknied in Congress two years before, and its essence is contained in Otis's pamphlet." To which Jefferson replied, "I know only that I turned to neither book nor pamphlet while writing it." [4]

When we recall that the first national copyright statute was enacted by the Congress of the United States in 1790 and that it remained for the twentieth century to permit "copyright" to signify "All rights reserved—no part of this book may be reproduced in any form without permission in writing from the publisher," [5] earlier writers must be more charitably judged than contemporary compilers. For certainly the day of manuscript and scribe is not comparable with the day of printed page and proofreaders.

To employ the concordance proof-text method to detect and demonstrate religious literary "theft" too often issues in absurdity. For example, in Isaiah 6 the prophet relates his call, his sense of mission, beginning with, "In the year that King Uzziah died, I saw also the Lord..." Mrs. Eddy knew Isaiah by heart.[6] Yet when she declares, "*In the year 1866, I* discovered *the* Christ Science..." she is not plagiarizing from Isaiah in spite of agreement in five words out of nine.

The problem of plagiarism is so intricate and complex, especially with reference to religious sources, that numerous illustrations should be cited to indicate its possibilities.

In Breasted's much-thumbed, excitingly interesting *History of the Ancient Egyptians*, the Ikhnaton religious revolution produced a hymn to Aton resembling Psalm 104.[7] The general trend of thought is similar. Yet in spite of the verbal identity in "how manifold are thy works," the Hebrew poet could not be indicted for plagiarism by any fair-minded grand jury, since for only seven verses out of thirty-five may parallels be discovered. Context may nullify verbal agreement and identical words centuries apart in time may have very different meanings. A concordance does not record changes in meanings of words wrought by semasiology. Two philosophers may employ identical words with different intentions. "Dialectic" does not have identical significance in Zeno, Plato, Aristotle, Kant, Hegel, Marx, Karl Barth, Dewey, Smith.

In the Fourth Eclogue of Virgil occur these beautiful lines:

> Lo the last age of Cumae's Seer has come
> Again the great millennial aeon dawns....
> E'en now thy brother, Lord of Light and Healing,
> Apollo, rules and ends the older day....
> The goats shall come uncalled, weighed down with milk
> Nor lions' roar affright the laboring kine....

28

> The treacherous snake and deadly herb shall die,
> And Syrian spikenard grow on every bank. . . .
> Nature shall give new colors to the fleece,
> Soft blushing glow of crimson, gold of crocus,
> And lambs be clothed in scarlet as they feed.

Employing the concordance proof-text method, one observes that "last age," "millennial aeon," "older day," "goats," "lion," "kine," "Syrian," "lambs," "fleece," are key words. Taking a Biblical concordance down from the shelf, it is a simple operation to accuse the Latin poet of "stealing" from Isaiah 11 and IV Ezra 4. For does not Isaiah say:

> And there shall come forth a shoot out of the stock of Jesse
> And the branch out of his roots shall bear fruit. . . .
> And the wolf shall dwell with the lamb,
> And the leopard shall lie down with the kid. . . .
> And the lion shall eat straw like the ox.

and IV Ezra 4:

> For the age is hastening fast to its end. . . .
> Then shall the sun suddenly shine forth by night and the moon
>   by day;
> And blood shall trickle forth from the wood, and the stone shall
>   utter its voice . . .
> The peoples shall be in consummation, the outgoings of the stars
>   shall change.

Here are agreements between the Roman Virgil and Hebrew writers in word and idea! "Plagiarism," of course! That IV Ezra was post-Virgil and Virgil never read Isaiah can be balanced, "you know," by the "faith of the church fathers," who let the Latin poet predict the birth of Jesus in these lines! Assuredly, then, Virgil stole ideas, phraseology and words from Hebrew writers, *quod erat demonstrandum!* And don't neglect the *must* in every gerundive including propaganda!

But the historical method now intervenes and demands to be heard. It denies the finding of the homiletical proof-text methods by insisting that although "it is remarkable that the poem was written at a time so near the birth of Christ, yet there seems no sufficient reason to connect the legends employed by Virgil with the proph-

29

ecies of the Old Testament. For the idea of the advent of a great and beneficent ruler of the world has been hardly less widespread than that of the coming of an age of peace. . . ." [8]

Even in case of complete verbal identity extending over many lines, immediate dependence of one writer upon the other may not be demonstrable. Take as illustration the oft-quoted words of Isaiah 2:1-4, the magnificent prediction of the coming age of peace and justice and internationalism.

The word that Isaiah the son of Amos saw concerning Judah and Jerusalem.

And it shall come to pass in the last days, that the mountain of the Lord's house shall be established in the top of the mountains and shall be exalted above the hills; and all nations shall flow into it.

And many people shall go and say, Come ye, and let us go up to the mountain of the Lord, to the house of the God of Jacob; and he will teach us of his ways, and we will walk in his paths: for out of Zion shall go forth the law, and the word of the Lord from Jerusalem.

And he shall judge among the nations, and shall rebuke many people: and they shall beat their swords into plowshares, and their spears into pruninghooks: nation shall not lift up sword against nation, neither shall they learn war any more.

But in Micah 4:1-3, the same passage is found. Did Isaiah "steal" from Micah? Did Micah "steal" from Isaiah? The passages assume the exile. Were they the expression of the people's hope? Were they originally composed by some late unknown poet? Did they become a *community hope* and thus find their way into the writings of two of the earlier writing prophets?

Who is the literary thief when psalms and portions of psalms are found to be identical? Psalm 14 is word for word identical with Psalm 53, except that the latter has *Elohim* for God consistently instead of *Yahweh*. In each instance later tradition ascribes it to David. But think of a modern hymnal repeating the same hymn within a few pages! Psalm 108 is composed verbatim of Psalm 57:8-12 and Psalm 60:7-14. Psalm 18 is of considerable length and reappears in II Samuel 22. Did the historian "steal" from the poet or the poet from the historian? Who was responsible for the identity of words found in II Chronicles 36:22 ff. and Ezra 1:1 ff.? Jeremiah 52:1-27 and II Kings 24:18 to 25:21 are identical. To assert

30

plagiarism in any of these instances would be to confess ignorance of methods of religious composition.

In the ancient world there were no copyright laws. In the modern world this earlier literary communism still survives in the unknown writers of newspaper editorials and in the anonymous reporters, in the compilers of almanacs and prayer and sermon manuals, in popular proverbs, in modern jokes smelling of pre-Christian make-up, in the *Congressional Record* where two congressmen on the same day within two hours make identical speeches,[9] in ghost writers for radio celebrities and for presidential candidates. But generally speaking, contact has now been lost with literature as communal property.

In ancient religious communities as well as in emerging religious dissenting groups at present the spoken word has magical potency. A "thus saith the Lord" silences all criticism. The world's foremost religious teachers through all the centuries have spoken their oracles and messages. The spoken formula produced the curse. The spoken anathema condemned to death.

Much later the spoken word was preserved in the archives of the tribe, in symbolic or written form, often with no author's name or scribe's identification attached to the cult emblem or literary deposit. The religious fellowship as such "owned" the saying or the address or the pronouncement. What individual could claim authorship when the developing book might be a series of tribal deposits extending over the centuries! Every generation had added its bit. The book was living, ever growing, ever expanding. In the Old Testament Psalter, "I" again and again is community utterance. The J document of the Pentateuch is the achievement of Judah and the E document is the achievement of Ephraim. Publication made the living volume a dead book.

"The entire Babylonian literature is anonymous." Hymns of Rig Veda are anonymous. Who sired folklore? There were only copyists, scribes then, not authors. What ancient languages had words for "author"? Particular words for speaker, orator, actor, teacher are not wanting in ancient vocabularies. But *scriptor* means copyist and *auctor* means creator, father, leader, teacher, founder, promoter, guardian, champion. Try to write "the *author* said" correctly for the twentieth century before our era. Back of the later words, Genesis, Exodus, Leviticus, Numbers, Deuteronomy, are the earlier words: First Book of Moses and so on. But still earlier Hebrew designations are: *in the beginning, names, and called, in the wilderness, words* for the first five volumes of the Hebrew Scriptures.

Because the written tradition preserved the oral tradition in more dependable form, it became holy literature in subsequent history, inerrant and unalterable, canonical, final for faith and practice. Thereupon the inherited anonymous books received names and titles. The originally anonymous Law has the name of Moses attached to it; the Psalter is associated with the name of David; Proverbs is assigned to Solomon and Koheleth as well. The David of history becomes the sweet singer of faith. Solomon, the tyrant of history who overtaxes his people for splendid building operations, becomes a wise man and a saint. Three sections of Proverbs were assigned to Solomon.

Jeremiah records the story of the composition of a roll thus:

And it came to pass in the fourth year of Jehoiakim the son of Josiah king of Judah, that this word came unto Jeremiah from the Lord, saying,

Take thee a roll of a book, and write therein all the words that I have spoken unto thee against Israel, and against Judah, and against all the nations, from the day I spake unto thee, from the days of Josiah, even unto this day.

It may be that the house of Judah will hear all the evil which I purpose to do unto them; that they may return every man from his evil way; that I may forgive their iniquity and their sin.

Then Jeremiah called Baruch the son of Neriah: and Baruch wrote from the mouth of Jeremiah all the words of the Lord, which he had spoken unto him, upon a roll of a book.[10]

In Ezekiel the transformation from speaking prophet to writing prophet is about complete.[11]

And after this, apocalypticism and all the other forms of Judaeo-Christian literary art and dependence appear.[12]

It does seem strangely inconsistent for orthodox ministers, then, to accuse the leaders of newer religious trends of plagiarism and the taking over of doctrines, when contemporary Christianity itself is such an amalgamation of extra-Jewish-Christian thinking and folklore with the "doctrines" of the Bible. The most "original" poets, philosophers, theologians, discoverers, inventors of recent years would be the first to admit their help from ages past. Christian thought is as stratified as the earth's crust.

The principal fallacies of bumbling homileticians who can "prove" that a statement in the religious literature of a dissenting body "must have been stolen" from one of the orthodox denominations are these: first, not to realize that orthodoxy has done some "stealing" and, second, completely to misunderstand how religious seers and prophets became and become convinced of their message.

The *visualization* of the divine and the holy by the prophet is the thing. Symbols are not imagined; they are seen. A cultus originates or is glorified or substantiated by natural ectasy or shock or fear. After the seen is reported, the priest interprets it into something in agreement with the group's theology. The symbol originates through an individual's "seeing" an ordinary thing or event in a new manner: Isaiah "SAW the Lord high and lifted up"; the author of the New Testament Apocalypse "SAW no temple" in the New Jerusalem. A primary symbol is revealed to the recipient in a moment of vision so that he or she is convinced. It is a uniquely experienced event. He believes because he has seen. He stores it in memory, begins to describe it to his group, and thus it becomes their faith. If, now, the symbol of one group is similar to the symbol of another group, no "theft" need be involved at all. Ten of the eleven major religions of the world have Golden Rules: did nine "steal" them? [13]

The vast Young *Analytical Concordance* that enables me to run down every idea of the Old Testament and the New Testament is as lifeless as the blotter on my desk. It becomes dynamic only when I become thrilled with the grandeur of the context in some passage in Amos, Hosea, Isaiah, Jeremiah, Luke, Romans, or Hebrews to which it has directed me. And our concordance-literalists might occasionally recall that hundreds of thousands of people have been sent on their way rejoicing through some revealing word which to them seemed stupid.

At first one may be simply staggered by the vast amount of minute and meticulous scholarship that it seems necessary to assume for all the comparisons made in the Haushalter book. One gasps with expectation of what new "proofs" will appear on the next page. But, then, fortunately, one may discover note 24 on page 79, which reads:

"*The Concordances* reveal some 340 references to 'idea' and

33

'ideal,' the majority of them in the sense used by Hegel." *"The Concordances"!* What a revelation of method! But there were so many short Hegelian expressions and words current in Europe and the United States that the concordance method of approach to the relationship between *Science and Health* and the alleged Lieber essay on *The Metaphysical Religion of Hegel* might lead one seriously astray.

And, finally, could not the "Lieber" essay be "stealing" from *Science and Health?* Does one build a large book upon a twelve-page essay or extract a twelve-page essay from a large book?

To return now from the accusation of literary piracy to the matter of the handwriting of the covering letter, the N.B. note, and the essay on Hegel.

In addition to the experts extraordinary in handwriting, Osborn and Stein, whose conclusions have been accepted by courts in the United States, various other handwriting authorities have refused to identify the handwriting of the "Lieber" writings with that of the historical Francis Lieber. They include historians, persons in governmental positions, librarians, students of ancient manuscripts.

A study of the photostat of the covering letter published in 1936 in "facsimile" with the Haushalter reproduction of the same year, yielded eighteen variations.[14]

A very careful comparison of the handwriting of the real Francis Lieber in 1865 and 1866 as to capital A's and capital S's with that of the "Lieber" manuscripts allegedly of the same period indicates that Lieber did not write the "Lieber" papers. In the course of his epistolary career, Lieber employed two kinds of A's and two kinds of S's. One A was written ⟨*A*⟩ ; the other, ⟨*A*⟩ . One S was written ⟨*S*⟩ ; the other, ⟨*S*⟩ .

If now a detailed examination is made of twenty-two genuine letters of Lieber between November 13, 1865, and April, 1866, the approximate period of the "Lieber" papers, the genuine letters of Lieber have no instance of ⟨*A*⟩ , but the "Lieber" materials have about one-third; the genuine Lieber letters have 45 instances of ⟨*A*⟩ , "Lieber" materials have no instances in covering letter, none in the title, 41 in the essay.

34

There are 58 instances of *∮* in the 22 genuine Lieber letters, November 3, 1865, to April 18, 1866; in the "Lieber" materials, none. There are 4 instances of *S* in the corresponding genuine Lieber letters; in the "Lieber" materials there are 3 instances in the covering letter, none in the title; about 122 in the essay.[15]

The handwriting issue seems to be going definitely in favor of "Lieber," not of Francis Lieber.

PART II

The "N.B." Notation

5

The Contents of the "N.B." Notation

THE title page presents problems too. How can the repetition of the peculiar and astounding twin-name "Francis Lieber-Christian Herrmann" absurdity on the title page be explained? Will the religious way out suggested in the covering letter do? Did it emerge after 1930 and demand the N.B. notation? Is the true-name-penname combination the key to the solution of the genuineness of the "Lieber" essay?

We recall that in the negotiations of 1930-1933 between the "solicitors" for the sale of the "Lieber" papers to the Directors of The Mother Church, no mention was made of an N. B. allegedly signed by Mary Baker and also no mention was apparently made of an author of the essay, Francis Lieber by name.[1]

Did these two, the authorship by Francis Lieber and the note signed "Mary Baker," enter the problem simultaneously? Did both put in an appearance about 1930?

The twin difficulty involved in the "Francis Lieber-Christian Herrmann" signature and the "Mary Baker" notation cannot be solved by quoting the alleged religious reason from the covering letter: "Read this paper under the pen-name Follen gave me 'Christian Herrmann.' I do not want my Professor title involved in religious controversy. Follen got a lesson there . . ."[2]

Lieber enjoyed religious controversy and had been involved in it from youth on. He dared to criticize his own "pastor." He reached sixty-six years of age in 1866 and had only six more years to go to 1872!

A brief summary of Lieber's attitude toward religion and his difficulties with the orthodox Christians is therefore pertinent at this

39

point. Personally pious, he manifested an inquisitive mind. He read the Koran and wrote upon Swedenborgianism and the Mormons.[3] He was "genuinely, if not conventionally religious." [4] The accusation of the orthodox that Lieber was an "infidel" is understandable when it is remembered that he opposed the Calvinism of the South.[5] He could characterize the Roman Catholic Church as "founded upon idolatrized Christianity." [6] He worshiped as a "liberal Episcopalian." [7]

In his personal *Commonplace Book*, Lieber bares his thoughts upon religion, God, the soul, and eternity as follows:

If God is God, he is almighty, all-comprehensive, omniscient, all-spiritual, etc. . . .

Thanks due to deity? If thanks, then he might have acted otherwise; then he has done something extra to us . . .

God created man in his own image in all his attributes except one, because the fact of creation forbade it. God is infinite love and mercy; we too can love and be merciful; he is omniscient and all-wise; we too can know and be wise, whatever folly our wisdom may be in his eyes. There is imprinted divinity in all of us. But creation absolutely divides God and man. He alone could make something out of nothing . . .

The concept of a personal God, and a belief in him, seems so natural to man, or rather so necessary a mould of his thoughts, that when he is bent on disavowing Him, his mind instantly and even unconsciously elevates something also, into a personality . . . Has this never been said before? I should wonder. I feel sure it has—by whom? . . .

From a practical point of view, Lieber proposed a number of suggestions for alterations of the Book of Common Prayer.[8] His private prayer book contains prayers for various occasions. He has one to be said after meals: "and gratefullly do we acknowledge that Thy Son has taught us to be thankful to Thee in the right way. Amen." [9] His prayer for a sick member of the family is quoted in full:

My God, Creator and Father of all men, I beseech Thee, in Thy wisdom, to heal and comfort the sick. In Thee I trust. Remove all danger and suffering, that we may all again serve Thee in health and strength, and each may joyously again perform the duties which Thou hast assigned to him, and vigourously pursue the path of wisdom, virtue and knowledge so that we may become more and more worthy of serving Thee in love toward Thee and one another. Amen.[10]

40

On the occasion of the death of a "little girl-friend," Lieber wrote a most touching letter to Ruggles, showing the same attitude as above:

But when those are draped in mourning we hear and acknowledge all the comfort which can be given and bow to God's decrees, and yet the heart continues to bleed and the eyes to weep. And it ought to be so; for there cannot be life without death, and, therefore, no love without grief. Nor can we help seeing that grief is a substantive element of the whole mental and moral and affectionate economy which our Maker has seen fit to establish for us. But since it is God who has done so, there must be wisdom and goodness in this checkered allotment, and there would be no goodness, but immeasurable and unspeakable cruelty were all to end here and were love of this world aught else than seed of flowers to bloom in heaven . . . My instincts, my feelings, lead me to believe that the departing only depart and that they perceive us. But who can know? I do know that death is not death, but death is life.[11]

Just how Francis Lieber, who had bravely defended his religion in the South for so many years, could fear to use his own name in the safer North and thereupon in hide-and-seek fashion sign it so abundantly in both covering letter and essay is so contradictory as to cause one to summon his ghost from the grave to explain the absurdity.

The religious reason for the use of a pen name in the "Lieber" essay will not suffice. Indeed, it could be argued that a man of such religious convictions could not possibly have broken with them so completely in the "Lieber" essay.

The N.B. reading on the title page: "This is Metaphysical Basis of Healing and Science of Health. Same as 'Christ-power and Truth-power,'" although signed "Mary Baker" was not written by Mrs. Eddy and is in the handwriting of the inventor of the "Lieber" essay.

To support the theory that Mrs. Eddy had written and signed the N.B., it was stated in an announcement published in 1947 by the editors of the Haushalter book: "1946, discovery [in Lyman P. Powell's authorized 'Mary Baker Eddy,' pp. 120, 121] of photostatic copies of two pages of Mrs. Eddy's handwriting, as of 1867, on almost identically ruled and lined commercial paper as that used by Francis Lieber in his 1865 document. Note *beneath* the pages:

'Notes of Instruction in Mrs. Eddy's handwriting given to her first student Hiram S. Crafts (1867).' " [12]

We have here samples of the handwriting of Mrs. Eddy and Mr. Crafts. But since Mrs. Mary Baker G. Eddy did not become Mrs. Eddy until January 1, 1877, that reference must be dated at least as late as that year. Besides, ledger paper like this could have been found in abundance by anyone seeking to create the appearance of a manuscript belonging to the period around 1866.

By calling attention to page 120 in the Powell biography of Mrs. Eddy, the editor-author has also helped to disprove in at least two ways his claim that the N.B. on the title page of the "Lieber" essay was written by Mrs. Eddy. For the signature in the N.B. is "Mary Baker." But in the 1860s her signature was "Mary M. Patterson," "M.M.P." "Mary M. P." Her divorce from Dr. Patterson was granted in 1873. And, further, the handwriting of the N.B. is definitely not that of Mrs. Eddy. A constant characteristic of Mrs. Eddy's handwriting is to slant the upward stroke of her below-the-line final consonants, such as "g" and "y" toward the right, for example, "*g*," "*g*," "*y*," "*y*," but never "*g*," "*y*." Yet in the N.B. signature, the slant is toward the left, "*Mary*"!

In Dresser's *The Quimby Manuscripts*, after page 440, several letters written by Mrs. Eddy appear in facsimile. The first is dated May 29, 1862, and the signature is "Mary M. Patterson" with the final "y" slanted in its upward final stroke to the right. The second letter is dated April 24, 1864, with the signature "M.M.P." The final "y"s in this letter likewise are slanted toward the right in their final upward stroke. Likewise in the remaining writings.

To summarize, in eighteen letters and poems, appearing in the Dresser volume, written between 1862 and 1866, of twenty signatures by Mrs. Eddy, there are ten instances of "Mary M. Patterson," four of "M.M.Patterson," and six of "M.M.P." No "Mary Baker" occurs and no final "y" has its final upward stroke bent to the left. Mrs. Eddy did not write the note at the bottom of the title page of the "Lieber" manuscripts.

But if results so definitely and completely contradictory to the claims of the editor or editors issue from a hasty, preliminary survey of the alleged N.B. on the title page of the "Lieber" essay, might not a study of the internal evidence in the covering letter and the essay itself issue in a reversal of the other conclusions reached by the collaborators both in the little blue book and in the "validation" of 1945 and the announcement of 1947?

As one rereads *Mrs. Eddy Purloins from Hegel* and begins to check its claims and to weigh its dogmatic conclusions, its inaccuracies, contradictions, mistakes, its failure to recover the original "Lieber" essays, its failure to double-check on scores of the trivial items that count so heavily in the final conclusion, the ignorance of its editors in matters German, philosophical, historical, and just plain common sense becomes oppressive.[13]

In Freidel's verdict upon the Haushalter volume quoted in the Foreword,[14] the historian writes: "The hand of the manuscript and of the alleged endorsement by Mary Baker Eddy, bear a marked resemblance." This identification of the scribe of essay and covering letter with the scribe of the N.B. notation is shared by handwriting experts who explain that the little difference in letter formations between it and the covering letter are due to the desire of the scribe to mislead the reader into assuming that "Mary Baker" was the author of the N.B. For example, the "y" of the N.B. in *metaphysical* and of the "g" in *healing* differ from these same letters in the covering letter.

But this cleverness did not pay off, because the scribe failed to remember the facts about the signature of Mrs. Eddy in this very year.

It might also be noticed that the paper used in the original numbered pages of the essay is conspicuous by its absence on the unnumbered title page.

It is also rather surprising to have such unusual attention centered upon the difference between "Christ-power" and "Truth-power" of the title page as compared with "Christ Power" and "Truth Power" of the covering letter:

Both these unusual hyphenated terms "Christ-power" and "Truth-power" Mrs. Eddy uses in her book *Science and Health*. It is worthy of note that Lieber did not connect either phrase with a hyphen.[15]

Such an ominous concern over a hyphen in the presence of the failure to record worry over: *Von der macht des gemuths den blossen vorsatz seines krankhaften gefuglemeister zu sein*—the biggest boner in American transcription of a well-known German title by Kant—allegedly written by Francis Lieber makes one marvel both at ability to discover the trivial and to pass by the significant.[18]

Before dealing with the main feature of this study, the "Lieber" essay itself, let us summarize what has been demonstrated thus far.

The key to the genuineness of "The Metaphysical Religion of Hegel" has already been found. If this were a mystery story, one of the clues would be the odd real name-alleged pen name-inseparable-combination appearing in the covering letter and continuing through title page and the essay to the last numbered page of the homily and note attached where it at last loses "Francis" and the pen name from the fixed, unalterable combination and diminishes to just plain "Lieber" in ridicule of the pen name. One desires to hide "Lieber" and so boldly puts him at the beginning and end of the brochure!

The second clue would be the N.B. on the title page, not written by Mrs. Eddy but by the scribe of these three documents in their present form. The disguise shines through.

The third clue would be the apparent lack of deep concern on the part of the associated authors to show that the present form of the writings existed from the year 1865 to the year 1936 or, to take the softer horn of the dilemma, from "the early eighties" to 1936—especially because such anxiety was manifested after 1936 over the matter of the failure to discover any historical Kantian Society, Boston Lyceum. A long research was conducted by a specially engaged expert to prove this and other assertions.

The fourth clue would be the failure to refute the published claim regarding the fact that apparently the names of both Francis Lieber and Mary Baker played no role in the negotiations of 1930-1933 for the sale of similar documents.

The fifth clue would be the strange faith in the religious reason advanced in the covering letter as accounting for the exceedingly absurd "Francis Lieber-Christian Herrmann" inseparably fixed combination, namely, that "Lieber" adopted this pen name, because he did "not want *his* Professor title involved in religious controversy. Follen got a lesson there"!

Hence, the provisional solution of the mystery up to this point might shape up something like this: Some person, possibly a student who had attended the Alcott-Harris school at Concord, observing rather remote possible similarities between this and that in New England transcendentalism, German-English-American idealism, in the post-eighties era, and *Science and Health*, for his own benefit pieced together a little composite essay. Years later this became the property of a Mr. X. Still later this attempt at interpretation of idealism was assigned to a German—"Christian Herrmann," shall we assume?

But an unknown "Christian Herrmann" would not attract customers. The massive two-volume work of Charles on the *Apocrypha* and *Pseudepigrapha* was by this time in print. And most theological students began to hear about the characteristics of "Apocalypse." One of these was *pseudonymity* and a particular brand of pseudonymity whereby a person like Daniel writing in 165/4 B.C. was represented as living in the sixth century B.C. Thus, he could "foretell" tolerably accurately the history of over three centuries.

If the existing brochure were antedated from the twentieth century to 1866 and assigned to the celebrated Francis Lieber in apocalyptic style, there would exist a noteworthy essay on Hegel by Francis Lieber.[17]

The rest was easy. The contents of the brochure could be distributed among the great German idealists giving the place of honor to the author's favorite Hegel but flanking him with Kant, Fichte, Schelling, Krause, Strauss, and some American names, including that of Mrs. Eddy.

But angry Clio was yet to be heard from in unmistakable repudiation of the unhistorical, apocalyptic procedure: "You have found some remote agreements between *Science and Health* on the one hand and this and that in New England transcendentalism and the various forms of nineteenth century idealism on the other. What you have failed to discern are the pronounced and radical differences between all of these. These universally acknowledged disagreements will be your undoing."

The third section of this inquiry will direct attention to these divergencies and will absolve both Francis Lieber and Mrs. Eddy from any connection with the "Lieber" brochure.

PART III

"The Metaphysical Religion of Hegel"

6

The Contents of the Essay

In the Haushalter study of the "Lieber" materials, there are found statements of Hegel's introduction to the United States:

Shortly thereafter [1832] his [Hegel's] influence began to penetrate Scotland and England, finding popular outflow through Carlyle and Coleridge. Toward the middle of the century Hegelianism won introduction to America through President Marsh of the University of Vermont, Emerson and Alcott in Boston, and by W. T. Harris, about 1862, in the *Journal of Speculative Philosophy* published in St. Louis, Missouri . . .[1]

The "Lieber" essay lets "Emerson, Channing and Parker" reflect "the Hegelian religion in America in their Unitarian views of Christ and atonement."[2]

The errors in these statements make it necessary to summarize the historical development of idealism in the United States. This can be done through recent critical studies in the areas of New England transcendentalism and Hegelianism.

Channing does not reflect the religion of Hegel and certainly precedes Emerson in time. His sermons are examples of sweet reasonableness and devotional appeal.[3]

Emerson's break with the orthodox Unitarian ministry came over sacramentalism. He was not a systematic theologian but a wise man and a prophet, defying classification. He was an optimist. He ethicized the problem of immortality He is skeptic, ethicist, mystic—all in one.[4] Emerson cared little for "schools," although he joined the Concord School of Philosophy in 1879. He never acquired "the dialectical proficiency requisite for a detailed comprehension and a complete assimilation" of Hegel. He read Harris's *Journal of Speculative Philosophy* rather uneasily. There was a chasm between Concord transcendentalism and St. Louis Hegelianism. Emerson played with it only "at arm's length" and once said:

> I cannot find any striking sentences in Hegel which I can take by themselves and quote. There is no period in him which rounds itself out into a detached thought, or pithy saying or remembrable metaphor... When I fish in Hegel, I cannot get a bite; in addition the labor is so hard in reading him, that I get a headache.[5]

Theodore Parker fought against Negro slavery and political corruption and demanded faith in God and the immortality of the soul, and his sermons are preached sometimes almost verbatim in orthodox Protestant pulpits today.[6] Parker had "a first hand knowledge of German philosophy on theology, was influenced by Strauss but not by Hegel directly." Strauss "went over from Hegelianism to pantheism." [7] It was in 1829 that "James Marsh called attention to German speculation by his American edition of Coleridge's *Aids to Reflection*." [8] but it did not take. The Bible, Plato, Aristotle, and Swedenborg were more to his liking than was Hegel. At the Concord School of Philosophy, 1879 to 1887, Alcott as titular head expounded Kant. Platonist Jones and Bronson Alcott "originally envisaged the school as a Platonic institution." W. T. Harris gained control and made it Hegelian. In 1881, at the third session, Harris gave ten lectures on Hegel; Jones, ten on Plato; Alcott shone at the Kant anniversary, finally crowning him "as the high-priest of 'Free Religionists,' 'Unitarians,' and 'Agnostics... and all that class.' " [9]

The *Journal of of Speculative Philosophy* was published between 1867 and 1888.[10]

This pointing up of the errors regarding Hegelianism and New England transcendentalism in the Haushalter volume must suffice as introduction to the analysis of "The Metaphysical Religion of Hegel."

Among the propositions to remember are: (1) American transcendentalism appears in the vicinity of Boston in an effective way in the 1830s and 1840s. (2) It was carried westward "by lectures, essays, reviews, books, young ministers, editors," and teachers.

(3) Centers of idealism appeared in Missouri and Illinois. (4) In St. Louis men like Brockmeyer, D. J. Snider, and W. T. Harris organized an Hegelian movement. (5) American idealism returned to Concord through the maneuvering of Alcott and Harris. (6) Through propagandists, notably Harris, it influenced the educational system of the United States. (7) American transcendentalism in its thesis form was Emersonian and Kantian; in its antithesis form in the East, Fichtean ethics plus the socialized religion of Schleiermacher and Rouge; in the West, there were Hegelian emphases; in its synthesis form at Concord, it attempted to integrate Alcott, Jones, W. T. Harris.[11]

With these general remarks upon the historical development of American idealism in mind, we turn now to a summary of those items in "The Metaphysical Religion of Hegel" which will enable us to reach dependable conclusions regarding its contents, its non-Hegelian character, its principal differences from Christian Science, its dependence upon *Science and Health*, the utter impossibility of its composition or transcription by Francis Lieber, and the deficiences in editorial comments.[12]

A commentary upon the entire "Lieber" essay would require discussion of many sentences not pertinent to our inquiry. Hence, we must be selective and direct attention merely to the more significant blunders.

To begin with, consider this paragraph:

Georg Wilhelm Friederich Hegel is the Copernicus for the new German metaphysics of religion. False science took no cognizance of the earth's motion and beheld the sun making a diurnal round. True science, contradicting false, taught the astronomer the sun is our solar center, and the earth turning on its axis revolves around it. Even as science through Copernicus destroyed Ptolemy's theory that earth is the center of the solar system and revealed the harmony of the spheres, so is it the mission of the German metaphysics by Hegel and his disciples to make an end to materialism by the philosophy of Spirit.[13]

This paragraph cannot possibly hail from Lieber under any circumstances and especially not when we read the eulogy on Strauss toward the end of the essay. For in *The Old Faith and the New* 1872, Strauss, *star pupil of Hegel*, created a big "sensation by his confession of materialism and atheism" (accusations long under discussion and at last frankly acknowledged), and from 1873 on, Mathilde Blind's English translation of Strauss was in the book-shops. Strauss alleges that modern cultured men are not Christians, that the faith he advocates needs neither a cultus nor a church, replaces the religious cultus with one of genius. Feuerbach, another pupil of Hegel, "like Strauss, ended at last in materialism"; "in his God, man knows himself only." And so the Feuerbach pun: "man is (*ist*) what he eats (*isst*)" survives.[14]

That the metaphysics of Hegel and some of his disciples did end in materialism is the view of Knox and Kroner, who put it thus: "David Friedrich Strauss, Ludwig Feuerbach, and men like them— Hegelians and also champions of anti-Christian materialism—show the nature and gravity of this danger [Hegel's dialectical recon-ciliation of reason and revelation] ... The history of the German mind in the nineteenth and twentieth centuries throws into relief the greatness of the danger. It was not only the banal and the shallow; at the end it was the brutal and the base that triumphed over the sublime. In his essay on 'Natural Law,' Hegel says that the man of excessive genius was a symptom of the inner disinte-gration and a portent of the approaching fall of Greek civiliza-tion. *The same might be said about* the great German thinkers, the greatest of whom was perhaps the author of *The Phenomenology of Mind*." [15]

It was while nineteen-year-old Karl Marx was reading Hegel's *Phenomenology of Mind* that he came to his crisis and wrote his father a letter containing "as I look upon life altogether *as the embodiment of a spiritual force* that seeks expression in every direction; in science, in art, and in one's own personality ... the individual's reason must proceed with its *self-contradiction* until it discovers its own unity. ... During my illness I had made ac-quaintance with Hegel from beginning to end as also with most of his disciples." [16]

It is difficult to understand how it can be successfully denied that Hegel profoundly influenced Karl Marx, and Thilly grants it: "What was once rational, Marx reasoned, becomes irrational in the process of evolution: private property ... once right and rational will be superseded and overcome as a result of the *dialectical-logical* process of history." [17]

Why did materialism appear in Germany? One answer has been

because of the flagging of the philosophic spirit and because the representatives of natural science fought so continuously against the conclusions of both Schelling and Hegel. The English naturalist could without going into a rage let scientific views run parallel to philosophico-religious interpretations while German naturalists felt that they must unify the world of material substances and mechanical motions with religious generalizations. Hence, psychical phenomena become vibrations of the brain and freedom of the will and all religious ideas became illusions.[18] So Marxism became economic Hegelianism.

But the Francis Lieber of history is described by Freidel as furious with the Marxists for daring to use his famous slogan "No Right without its Duty; No Duty without its Right" upon their banners. He discerned in 1851 that the extreme despotism in Russia would "create ultimately a convulsive explosion and give for a time, fearful power to Communism, Socialism and all other sorts of freak democratic absolutism." [19]

But if Lieber had known Hegelian dialectics he should either have violently rejected its application to economics or have discovered its "spiritual" significance. He did neither.

In his word about J. G. Fichte, "Lieber" lets Fichte "pass away" in 1812 instead of 1814 and Hegel in 1832 instead of 1831 and then purports to quote from Fichte:

In his *Vocation of Man* (*Die Bestimmung des Menschen*) Fichte says as follows: "The historical is fact, the metaphysical, higher Law. Historical fact becomes metaphysics by the transcendental Understanding. In man dwells the image of true Being. When man's visible being is harmonious with the Ideal all is well for him. Complete truth is Science and the essence of the Science of Being is Reflection. There is but one way to harmony, to have no other consciousness of life than God and His Reflection." [20]

Since nothing resembling this is found in the Smith translation, could it possibly have originated in the fertile mind of "Lieber" or have been mistakenly transferred to Fichte by his source?

A little error regarding the publication of Hegel's works *immediately* after his death in November of 1831 implies composition of the essay at a much later date than 1865. "Lieber's" comment reads: "The works of Georg Hegel were published in in eighteen large volumes *just after* his death (1832) by Duncker and Humblot in Berlin. Good fortune has not yet translated them for American readers." [21]

But the Verlag of Duncker and Humblot did not publish the works of Hegel in 1832 in eighteen large volumes. It only began to do so. Volume 17, for example, was published in 1835; volume 18 in 1840, part I of volume 7 in 1842; part II in 1845. Any American scholar who had waited a decade and one-half for a particular volume would not have described the edition as appearing "just after" the death of Hegel in 1831. Such an erroneous statement visualizes the mistaken author of it before a card catalogue of, let's say, the twentieth century.

Moreover, it is now established that in the complete edition of Hegel's lectures and works, friends and students included *unpublished* materials. They added those concerned with logic, with natural philosophy, with the doctrine of the subjective spirit to the corresponding sections in the *Encyclopedia* or to the *Rechtsphilosophie* in case of the doctrine of the objective spirit. Sometimes they even independently revised his lectures. This was the case in regard to the *Philosophy of History*, the *Aesthetics*, the *Philosophy of Religion*, and the *History of Philosophy*. His *Philosophische Propaedeutik* prepared for the *Nürnberger Unterricht* was likewise printed in this complete edition.

Since these independently student-edited-and-revised materials whose authenticity in detail is in question were used by the "Lieber" allegedly associated with "The Metaphysical Religion of Hegel," it is rather difficult to understand how the editor-author of the Haushalter book can be so certain he is dealing with undoubted Hegel materials in the purchased essay. For on page 76 of this book, "Lieber" writes: "The passages quoted in this paper are my own translations from the *Philosophie der Religion*, *Aesthetik*, *Wissenschaft der Logik*, and *Philosophie der Geschichte*."

Moreover, in 1907, Herman Nohl published Hegel's *Theologische Jugendschriften* and, in 1948, Knox and Kroner published *Georg Wilhelm Friedrich Hegel, Early Theological Writings*, where on pages 331-334 in a bibliographical note section C, *Lectures Published by his Pupils after Hegel's Death*, it is said: "... two facts about the lectures must be borne in mind: (a) They were not published by Hegel himself, and their authenticity in detail is not beyond doubt; (b) the translations are based upon the text, now partly obsolete, of the first edition of Hegel's collected works (19 vols.; Berlin, 1832-45 and 1887, reprinted with few changes as *Jubilaeumsausgabe*, 20 vols.; Stuttgart, 1927-30)." [22]

Hence the author of "The Metaphysical Religion of Hegel" claims to have based his essay upon the very works which the master had not prepared for publication and was substituting student memory and revision for Hegel. What contemporary professor would care to be charged with saying what is found in student notebooks? The case for even the authenticity of the Hegelian quotations in "The Metaphysical Religion of Hegel," some 188 lines, is thus much impaired.

The writings published by Hegel himself available in translation are: *Phenomenology of Mind, The Science of Logic, Encyclopedia of Philosophical Sciences in Outline,* and *Philosophy of Mind* of which two and three are out of print. [23]

"Lieber" now comes to grips with the essentials of Hegelianism:

The first step to understand Hegel is the "Idea." He says the world would collapse without intelligence and its Ideas. "All that is has truth only when it is a definite existent Idea. The Idea is the only truly real. The Idea is truth in virtue of its essential Being and fundamental principle. It is not sensuous, corporeal existence but the Idea is universal. Yet the Idea seeks realization in external nature through Mind." "The final Idea is Mind, Spirit. This Spirit is not finite and limited to sense but universal and absolute which by its own action determines truth. The appearance of nature is what Mind sets up as product. Nature as object of Mind owes to Spirit the gift of essential substance. Nature is set up as a creation of the Idea by Mind." *(Aesthetik)* [24]

The Lieber of history was a scholar for whom such inexact references and all the inexact references in the succeeding pages would be humiliating.

Yes, with Hegel "reality is embodied only in the Idea, eternal, self-developing, ever-growing by its own process of dialectical contradiction: thesis, antithesis, synthesis. The Idea incorporates itself with nature, expresses itself in phenomena, and fills the human mind with images and ideas. The material world is but an expression of the Absolute Idea."

If only once in the entire essay "Lieber" had introduced the notion of contradiction to imperfect thesis and thus started the dynamic dialectical process, the reader might feel he was reading a serious analysis of Hegelian philosophy instead of a homily.

Wilhelm Windelband states that Hegel

assumes that in the development of the human spirit the absolute spirit itself finds the highest development. In Hegel's philosophy of history, philosophy of religion, history of philosophy, the human spirit of culture not only bears the name of world spirit but is actually regarded as such. The necessary developmental forms of the human spirit are those of the universe. Hegel's absolute Spirit is actually the human spirit. . . . If human thought is measured only by itself, if it is really the absolute, then its own inherent development is also the truth. The psychological necessity of human thought demands that its development consists of originating ideas, letting them be transformed into one another. The dialectic with its contradictions and its indefinite transformations of imagined content is the naturally necessary character of human thinking. The dialectic method consists of exchanging this psychologically necessary process with the logical. The psychological antithetical movement of the *Vorstellungen* therefore turns itself into a real conflict and reconciling process of the imagined content. For it, the negation and the antithesis have metaphysical significance and its inherent restlessly creating and again disintegrating movements projects it into a *Weltanschauung* of eternal becoming.[25]

But precise reference to this dialectical process is totally missing from homilist "Lieber's" sermon.

There is a passage in "The Metaphysical Religion of Hegel" where the author of the Haushalter volume simply cannot restrain himself sufficiently to put the results of his research into a footnote but must introduce it into the "Lieber" text:

That man epitomizes the universe, and is the body of God is apparent not only from the logic of truth but in the phenomenon before the spiritual senses. In the words of Pope [Even these words of Pope are reproduced by Mrs. Eddy in S. & H., 1st, ed.]

"All are but parts of one stupendous whole.
Whose body nature is, and God the soul." [26]

Mrs. Eddy must have taken her two lines quoted from Pope's *Essay on Man* from "Lieber's" little dissertation on Hegel! *Nothing could be less true!*

Mary Baker was as familiar with Lindley Murray's *English Reader* as with the *Westminister Catechism*. At the age of nine she was reading both the Murray *Introduction to the English Reader* and the *English Reader* itself over and over again. There were over four hundred pages in the two books. The best English writers were quoted in them—Goldsmith had over twenty pages; Addison, twenty-one; Thompson, over ten; Pope, *over nine;* Cowper, over seven; Samuel Johnson, over seven; Hume, over five; Milton, over four; Young, four; More, three; Benjamin Franklin, two pages. Greek and Roman writers who appeared in good translations included Socrates, Plato, Horace, Sallust, Cicero, Marcus Aurelius. The Bible in the King James text appeared in the *Readers* in abundance.[27]

As far as the famous couplet from Pope is concerned, it had been printed again and again and again in many pamphlets, calendars, primers for decades before Mary Baker Eddy's day. Why, then, was Mr. Haushalter so invincibly certain that Mrs. Eddy took it from "Lieber's" Hegelian brochure particularly when this dissertation had not as yet been composed? To end all this "heavy" research, turn to page 241 of Lindley Murray's *English Reader* in the edition of 1823. What readest thou?

> All are but parts of one stupendous whole,
> Whose body nature is, and God the soul.[28]

There are similar "discoveries" by the compilers of the Hegel materials which are very exciting. One is met with in this "Lieber" reference to "apodictical":

This grand apodictical principle which Hegel thus sets forth so brilliantly in *Aesthetik* reaches its height in the *Logik . . .*[29]

It receives at last three comments with the help of the concordance of *Science and Health* in such constant use. It well illustrates one of the weaknesses of the concordance method, namely, its obliteration of semasiology and its failure to allow for nearer sources of verbal identities than plagiarism.

Philosophical conclusions sometimes get into the popular vocabulary. School readers, selections of readings from larger works, digests of magazine articles, may be the source of a quote instead of a heavy tome. Very few persons have read the Bible from cover to cover but they have heard a minister or a Sunday-school teacher quote an apt phrase and it became their own. Students do search for I Corinthians 13 in the Old Testament but a few can *say* "And now abideth faith, hope, charity, these three; but the greatest of these is charity." They can recite the Lord's Prayer without being able to find it in Matthew. A McGuffey Reader might be the remote source and a bright child's photographic memory the immediate source of a quotation from Shakespeare instead of a critical edition of *The Merchant of Venice*.

Let the editor now relate his find:

With the use of such terms as "apodictical," "ontology," "identity," "monad," "metaphysics," "science of being,"—phrases direct from the vocabulary of Hegelian Idealism,—the wonderment arises how Mrs. Eddy could have convinced herself that the Bible was her only source of inspiration! [30]

And, again, Mrs. Eddy used such words as " 'apodictical,' a term coined by Kant." [31]

The editor is very fond of this discovery, for on the third occasion he is even more emphatic. He supplies a note after quoting from *Science and Health*:

This apodictical Principle points to the revelation of Immanuel, "God with us,"—the sovereign ever-presence, delivering the children of men from every ill "that flesh is heir to." (*Science and Health*, p. 107: 7-10) [32]

But "apodictical" occurs at least as early as A.D. 1615 and frequently thereafter. Kant was born in A.D. 1724.

"We have not been able to find that the word 'apodictical' was used in the First Edition of *Science and Health with Key to the Scriptures* by Mary Baker Eddy." Hence, the author of "The Metaphysical Religion of Hegel" was quoting from a post-1875 edition of *Science and Health*. Yet Mrs. Eddy is supposed to have seen the "Lieber" essay in 1866.

Also on page 76, the editor admits by implication that he is using a later edition of *Science and Health* than the first when he quotes:

Ontology is defined as "the science of the necessary constituents and relations of all beings," and it underlies all metaphysical practice. [33]

For the page quoted from *Science and Health* is 460. Mrs. Eddy is supposed to have read the "Lieber" essay in 1866! Why is the 1875 edition not quoted?

The theory of the dependence of "The Metaphysical Religion of Hegel" upon *Science and Health* is gaining in credibility apparently.

The word "ontology" existed in the sixteenth century and was popularized by Christian Wolff and his school. The ontological argument appears in Descartes, Spinoza, Leibnitz. In fact, does not Anselm advance a modified ontological argument for the existence of God? [34]

Likewise, the word "identity" is older than German idealism, being found in Locke, who died in 1704, and in Spinoza, almost three decades earlier. And "monad" was used by Giordano Bruno, Leibnitz, and Wolff. Leibnitz found it in von Helmolt, who died in 1699.[35]

One of the most fantastic passages in the brochure under examination is this alleged title of an essay by Kant:

Von der macht des gemuths den blossen vorsatz seiner krankhaften gefuglemeister zu sein.[36]

Not one of the German scholars consulted could do anything with this but all asserted that Francis Lieber could not have composed it, copied it, or dreamed it. Apparently even the editor could not explain this one, since he offers no comment. It takes first prize for stupidity. There are ten mistakes here in thirteen German words: omission of five capital letters and two umlauts plus the word *durch* with *Gefuehle* changed to *gefugle* and combined with *Meister*. For all this blundering, "no comment"! This is astounding! This German title makes no sense. It does not parse. There is no footnote to unravel the tangled skein. *No German wrote this.* Not even a dozing, weary "Lieber" could have written this Kantian title.

When one first reads this, one sits and stares at the translation into German, thinking it may be another instance of glaring error and "hog German" due to the editor's or the printer's misunderstanding. On consulting page 9 of the facsimile and comparing it with page 100 of the Haushalter reproduction, however, one notices that the editor only added the italics to both the English and German titles but failed to record that even the anonymous scribe was having his troubles, deleting *Mastery* and then copying it again as Self-Mastery. So, on the whole, this one is on the house!

Far away from a library we read and reread this Kantian title. It was not in our dependable Falckenberg. Late in January, 1949, we were beginning to get some results through correspondence with Professor E. P. Appelt, the head of the German Department in the University of Rochester. He had been very cooperative and had found the correct title of the Kantian essay: It is: *Von der Macht des Gemüths durch den bloszen Vorsatz seiner krankhaften Gefühle Meister zu sein.* What the original literary inventor had written, no one knows. But the copyist knew so little German that he produced the atrocious concoction now in the "Lieber" essay. Francis Lieber could not have been guilty of this mutilation of his mother tongue. *And the editor just reprinted it without comment!* This is "no comment" with a vengeance.

The essay of Kant originally appeared in Hufeland's *Journal fuer die praktische Heilkunde* in 1797.[37] It was reprinted several times and in 1868 appeared in the seventh volume of G. Hartenstein's edition of Immanuel Kant's *Saemmtliche Werke in Chronologische Reihenfolge,*[38] where it was printed on pages 409 to 428. Observe that this edition of Kant dates from after the date of the alleged covering letter, April 1, 1866.

The reference in the "Lieber" essay to the Kant composition on the power of mind over body is very apt. For his day, Kant was pioneering in the matter of health and physical culture. Kant's diagnosis of health is listed under *Der Streit der philosophischen Facultaet mit der Medicinischen* (The Controversy between the Philosophical and Medical Faculties) in Hartenstein. It is the third section in the conflict between the faculties, the preceding two sections being: (1) The conflict between philosophy and theology; (2) the conflict between philosophy and law. It was a rejoinder addressed to *Herrn Hofrath und Professor Hufeland.* In the latter half of the nineteenth century numerous editions of this essay were printed in Germany. In England, Sir J. Sinclair edited a translation of Kant's works printed in 1807 and this essay appeared under the title of *The Code of Health and Longevity* in volume 3, on page 245. Its translator was J. C. Colquhoun. The library of Columbia University in the City of New York has twenty-one editions of this Kantian essay published between 1798 and 1881. Colquhoun translated the German title into *On the power of the mind in overcoming unpleasant sensations by mere resolution.*[39]

The 1834 edition of *Encyclopedia Americana*, a work of the Lieber of history, states that "Hufeland, the physician, published Kant's work, *Of the Power of the Mind by Mere Resolution to control its Morbid Feelings, with notes.*"[40]

Hence, there was an elaborate article by Kant upon the power of the mind, making use of only will and desire, to master neuroses. Had the compiler of "The Metaphysical Religion of Hegel" read it, would he not have added at least an explanatory comment? Instead, he wrote down in English its misunderstood but approximate title as "The Power of Mind Through Sheer Self-Mastery to Overcome Illness" after having perpetrated an atrocious literary crime by copying the fantastic German title maligning Kant.

Yet even the copyist was bewildered.[41] In copying the English title before his eyes, he deleted the word "mastery" and rewrote "self-mastery," but obtained only a partially correct English title for the Kantian essay.

The final evidence in this magnificent blunder to show that the Lieber of history could not have written this dissertation on "Hegel" is supplied by a comparison of "Lieber's" translation of the title of Kant's treatise on health as found in "The Metaphysical Religion of Hegel" and the real Lieber's translation of the title of the same essay, as found in the 1834 article on Kant in his *Encyclopedia Americana:*

Page 100 of the "Lieber" Essay	Volume VII, page 306 (1834)
The Power of Mind Through Sheer Self-mastery to Overcome Illness.	*Of the Power of the Mind by Mere Resolution to Control its Morbid Feelings.*

Why did not the "Lieber" of the essay merely turn to the Lieber translation of 1834 in the *Encyclopedia Americana* to save himself the trouble of contradicting himself in "1865"?

After 1875 there was a Kantian revival which came into full swing in the 1880s and the mention of Feuchtersleben[42] and Krause with Kant on page 100 of the essay may reflect this situation. There were several Krauses—Friedrich, Ernst, and Albrecht. The description is too indefinite and vague to reach any conclusion. The reader passes from Hegel to Kant to Feuchtersleben to Krause to Hegel with too little particular material for valid judgment. Albrecht Krause was writing in defense of Kant in the eighties! Some of his statements may form "Lieber's" background here. If so, the implications of the essay would demand a post-1885 date.[43]

According to "Lieber," Hegel's view regarding evil is "on the lines of Baader and the theodicy of Leibniz."[44] Franz von Baader turned from Kant to the theosophy of Saint-Martin and Jacob Boehme. "A lively imagination was apt to get the upper hand of sober critical understanding; he suffered from the want of logical self-control ... quite incapable of treating the subject in a connected way, constantly leaping from theme in hand to another quite remote from it; and leaping also away from thought altogether to the spinning of fancies and mythologies. *This makes it uncommonly difficult to describe Baader's philosophy.*" Baader regarded a "free" philosophy "founded on the authority of Catholic tradition" as the cure for the evils of the age![45]

"Lieber" seems to be using a homiletical sounding board again. It would have been very difficult for the Lieber of history to ponder the fifteen volumes of Franz von Baader in which neo-Platonism, Augustine, Thomas Aquinas, Meister Eckhart, Paracelsus, Jacob Boehme, Kant, Fichte and so on, appear for comment.

Gottfried Wilhelm Leibnitz (1646-1716) in the theodicy addresses himself to the problem *si Deus est, unde malum*[46] thus:

God could certainly have brought into actuality a world in which there would have been less imperfection than in ours, but it would at the same time have contained fewer perfections. No world whatever can exist entirely free from evil, entirely without limitation—whoever forbids God to create imperfect beings forbids him to create a world at all ...

Such an authority as Falckenberg does not agree that the Hegel and Leibnitz views of evil may be equated:

In the Leibnitzian theodicy the least satisfactory part is the justification of moral evil. *We miss the view defended in such grand outlines by Hegel, and so ingeniously by Fechner, that the good is not the flower of a quiet, unmolested development, but the fruit of energetic labor;* that it has need of its opposite; that it not merely must approve itself in the battle against evil without and within the acting subject, but that it is only through this conflict that it is attainable at all. Virtue implies force of will as well as purity, and force develops only by resistance. Although he does not appreciate the full depth of the significance of pain, Leibnitz's view of suffering deserves more approval than his questionable application to the ethical sphere of the quantitative view of the world, with its interpretation of evil as merely undeveloped good. But, in any case, the compassionate contempt of the pessimism of the day for the "shallow" Leibnitz is most unjustifiable.[47]

A sentence or two in "The Metaphysical Religion of Hegel" is contradictory to the historical Lieber's attitude toward his adopted country. For he early identified himself with the United States, became a citizen, and was not inclined to assert the superiority of Germany:

Also many who judge Hegel do it by what we call in Germany *Kamin-Philosophie (Parlour-fire Philosophy)* [Italics inserted in Haushalter reproduction]. These shallow people charge that Hegel makes Man God [declares the "Lieber" of the essay].[48]

This may, of course, also have been an attempt on the part of the final scribe to imitate the Germanicisms of Francis Lieber and convince the reader that the essay was not a forgery.

"The Metaphysical Religion of Hegel" calls his doctrine of immortality "the supreme climax of all that the metaphysics of Hegel declares concerning God and Man." [49] He devotes over forty lines to it and boldly claims that it "places Hegel in the forefront of the world of thinkers of all time." [50] This discussion is rather interesting compared with the remainder of this "Lieber" essay. The trite, the commonplace, the superficial, and the shopworn arguments for immortality are of course conspicuous by their presence. If this is all Hegel has to offer regarding the immortality of the soul, his heavy thinking has hardly added to the agelong discussion of the problem. The interesting emphases appear where "Lieber" leans on *Science and Health.*

For, according to "Lieber," immortality is a present quality of the human spirit—nothing new here, of course! Heaven is not a "local habitation" but the harmony of mind and body. He probably is not complaining about life in New York City and Washington. Socrates "pledged the superiority of Spirit over matter in a cup of hemlock poison"—is that what Socrates did? Because man is *imago Dei*, he is a reflection of God, that is, $1 = 1$! Man ought not to "pollute the motives of conduct by rewards of heaven and penalties of hell"—to think that "Lieber" could turn the beautiful sentence "Sin makes its own hell, and goodness its own heaven" (*Science and Health* 196:18, 19) into that!

What occasions surprise is that "Lieber" asserts that Hegel reaches the climax of his thought in his doctrine of immortality. For it is a historic fact that when Hegel died his lectures on immortality were one of the reasons for the schism among his students and their division into left-wing and right-wing Hegelians. His own students were in doubt as to the Meister's views regarding the immortality of the soul. Was it the "individual existence on the part of particular spirits, or only the eternity of the universal reason"? But the Francis Lieber of history was genuinely orthodox in regard to the hope of immortality. Another puzzling matter in these two paragraphs is that "Lieber" devoted only one-fourth of his space to Hegel quotations on immortality!

"Lieber" quotes only briefly an unimportant sentence or two from *Aesthetik* and apparently eight short sentences from *Philosophie der Religion*. The latter quotations, when examined for accuracy, reveal the same carelessness in rendering as have characterized all tested quotes in this essay. For example, "Lieber" renders: "The immortality of the soul is not to be described as coming to reality only at a future stage; it is present nature of Spirit. Spirit as eternal is always present. The everlastingness of Spirit is brought to consciousness and is no longer enmeshed in the finite, external, natural."

What Hegel wrote was:

"So muss bei der unsterblichkeit der Seele nicht vorgestellt werden, dass sie erst spaeter in wirklichkeit trete; sie ist gegenwaertige Qualitaet. Der Geist ist ewig, also, deshalb schon gegenwaertig. Der Geist in seiner Freiheit ist nicht im Kreise der Beschraenktheit. Fuer ihn als denkend, rein wissend ist das Allgemeine Gegenstand—dies ist die Ewigkeit. Die Ewigkeit des Geistes ist hier zum Bewusstsein gebracht in diesem Erkennen, in dieser Trennung selbst, die zur Unendlichkeit des Fuersichseins gekommen ist, die nicht mehr verwickelt ist in natuerliches, zufaelliges, aeuszeres." [51]

64

Thirteen lines of Hegel cannot be reduced to five lines of "Lieber" without serious injury to the context! In this "Lieber" quotation the Hegelian dialectic that is the heart of the matter vanishes and so *zufaelliges* can actually be transformed into *finite!*

We also feel that Mrs. Eddy's "Because he understood the superiority and immortality of good, Socrates feared not the hemlock poison" is a thousand paces ahead of "Lieber": "Socrates understood this when pledging the superiority of Spirit over matter in a cup of hemlock poison ..." Again, "Lieber" is the "purloiner."

As far as Hegel's views on immortality are concerned, here are some of them:

... Even his [Abraham's] hope of posterity—the one mode of extending his being, the one mode of immortality he knew and hoped for—could depress him...[52]

... How could they [the Jews] have hoped even for the poor immortality in which the consciousness of the individual is preserved...[53]

... Where we [modern Christians] have intellectual cognition of a determinate fact or a historical objectivity, they [early Christians] often see spirit; where we [modern Christians] place only spirit unalloyed, there they [early Christians] look on spirit as embodied. An instance of the latter type of outlook is their [early Christians'] way of taking what we call immortality and in particular the immortality of the soul. To them it appears as a resurrection of the body. Both outlooks are extremes, and the Greek spirit lies between them.... For both extremes, death is a separation of body and soul; in the one case the body of the soul exists no longer, in the other, the body is a persistent, though here too it is without life.[54]

"Lieber" seems to have derived some of his views on the immortality of the soul from a study of *Science and Health* rather than from any reflections of Hegel's. *Moreover, these materials "Lieber" does not assign to Hegel.* The author-editor of the little blue book does that. "Lieber" apparently had *Science and Health* opened to the proper pages as he wrote. For example, "Heaven is not a locality, but a divine state of Mind in which all the manifestations of Mind are harmonious and immortal..." (291:13-16) is far more original than "Lieber's" "heaven is not a local habitation." Both Hegel and "Lieber" were incapable of originating *Science and Health*, page 81:17-30.

At page 105 of the Haushalter reproduction of the "Lieber"

essay on Hegel,[55] its inventor begins a short digression on David Friedrich Strauss and Hase with passing reference to Emerson, Channing, Parker, and Orelli of Zürich. There are errors here which one would not be inclined to assign to Francis Lieber.[56] Often they do not concern the main issue of this study.

As an illustration of the faulty method of "Lieber" in dealing with quotes to establish a point, the following instance suffices:

So also says Strauss. "The miracles in the sense of the old popular belief cannot be of any particular value. We do not think much of them, only because to us they are lost, like a drop in the ocean, amongst the innumerable wonders which God is daily and hourly performing in all parts of the world created and supported by him." *(Letter to Orelli)*

The above quotation ascribed to Strauss not only quotes it out of context but fails to indicate that after the word "value," which in the original is followed by a comma not a period, five and one-half necessary lines are omitted. Hence, our "Lieber" has again missed Strauss' point.

We first quote what "Lieber" has omitted after the word "value":

but to him who is unable to discover the power and wisdom of the Creator in the natural regulation of the world; and we, who are accused of not believing in those miracles which God performed in Judea at the time of Moses and the prophets—of Jesus and the apostles—we do not think ...

Now, for context, a page preceding the beginning of Strauss' quote should be cited as well as the materials following "supported by him." Only several sentences of the latter follow here:

You will find it particularly elevating that Christ has twice fed thousands of people with a small provision through the power of his Father. What, only twice! and a long time ago, has *your God* been doing what *ours* is doing every year—yea every day.... In short, you cannot mention any miracle which we have not also and even greater and more splendid.

Strauss is explaining to the ordinary people of Zürich that their pastors have not pointed out to them that heretic Strauss has merely made all nature and the life of man a continuous miracle. Instead of experiencing miracle only in the extraordinary events of life, he suggests that they find it in every experience of joy and pain. The Father knows the needs of men long before they do and feeds the birds of the air by providing them with sharp eyes and strong wings so that they can thus supply their own needs.

After Hegel's death, there were three points at issue regarding his views: theism, personal immortality, and the interpretation of Jesus.[57] His conservative students maintained that Hegel was orthodox; his liberal students, like Ruge, Richter, Bever, Strauss, and Feuerbach, held that Hegel taught that God becomes consciousness in humanity, that universal mind is eternal, and that Jesus is an expression of the divine in humanity.[58] Royce has observed that "while the original Hegelian school ultimately lost its direct influence in Germany, the indirect influence of the Hegelian system still remains very great and is especially noticeable in *English and American thought since 1865.*"

Strauss went to Berlin to meet Hegel. The meeting occurred just before the cholera suddenly took Hegel in 1831. The next year Strauss was a brilliant lecturer in philosophy at Tübingen. When his *Leben Jesu* appeared in June, 1835, his position at Tübingen went by the board. The violence at Zürich closed his academic career. His marriage to the songster Agnes Schebert proved unfortunate. Strauss wandered from city to city settling in his home town, Ludwigsburg, at sixty-four years of age. His pioneering *Life of Jesus* applied Hegelian philosophy to the gospel story consistently from the childhood stories to resurrection and ascension. Strauss did not question the historicity of Jesus. His critical analysis was without synthetic reconstruction. People asked, as always, whether anything remained. The 27-year-old author thrice defended his thesis and in the third edition, 1838, made amazing concessions to his critics but canceled them out in the fourth edition, on which the English translation was based.[59]

In his *Die Christliche Glaubenslehre* (1841), Strauss made faith antithetical to knowledge, *revising Hegel.* In 1848 he supported the state and in 1870 he defended Bismarck's diplomacy. His *Das Leben Jesu fuer das deutsche Volk* (1864),[60] with its distinction between the Christ of faith and the Jesus of history, was a criticism of Schleiermacher. His *Die Halben und die Ganzen* (1865) and *The Old and the New Faith* (1872), plus an *Addendum* in which Strauss *abandoned much Hegelianism by subscribing to dogmatic materialism and by attempting to be two in one, both mate-*

rialist and idealist, ended the thinking of a bold, honest scholar and brought back the earlier tornado of criticism.[61] In *The Old and the New Faith,* translated by Mathilde Blind in 1873, Strauss answers two primary questions. To "Are we still Christians?" he replies "No"; to "Have we still a religion?" his answer is "Yes," if understood in the ethical and aesthetic sense. Myth is "suprasensible fact presented in the form of history and symbolic language." Myths possess speculative absolute truth but have no historical reality.

Horace Friess has observed that Strauss "definitely rejected the view that the truth of Christian dogma could be reestablished by speculative idealism. According to Strauss modern philosophy culminates in a humanistic pantheism, which can give new religious satisfaction but the content of which is not, as Hegel claimed, identical with Christianity. Not the unique man-God, Jesus, but the divinity of humanity in its consciousness of the universe is its central conception." [62]

Karl August von Hase (1800-1890) also is not too well known by "Lieber." Hase reflects the varied political, philosophical, artistic, theological, and ecclesiastical trends of the nineteenth century. He was dismissed from both Leipzig and Erlangen, for participation in *Burschenschaft* activities. He criticized Schelling and did not blindly approve Schleiermacher's conclusions. The romantic trend influenced him. He felt his call to be to unite rationalism with romanticism and "warmth of heart." Neo-pietism, Hase contended, did not represent original Protestantism. He participated in the *Kulturkampf* against Roman Catholicism. Hase was really a mediating theologian, defending to some extent religious supernaturalism. He was a loyal coworker with ecclesiastical liberalism. Hase's fame rests upon his achievements as a church historian. In this area he sought to introduce a vital understanding of the trend of events, emphasized composition of monographs and the study of Christian art. "Lieber's" reference to Hase is below average.[63]

"Lieber" concludes his brochure on "The Metaphysical Religion of Hegel" with: "Religion is the knowledge of the Divine Spirit through mediation of finite spirit. Thus the highest mode of the Idea makes religion not an invention of man, but the lofty determination of the Absolute itself." [64]

68

And for this Mr. Haushalter does not seem to have found a single parallel in any edition of *Science and Health*.

Here is the very interesting close of the "Lieber" document:

Francis Lieber   *"Christian Herrmann"*
(Copy in Portfolio Columbia)
           Written November 1865
           Copied for Hiram Crafts
           Kantian Society April 1866

What could the original of "Lieber" have meant by this one? Where was the original manuscript of the little essay supposed to be? Since a copy was "in portfolio Columbia," why didn't it show up in the literary remains of "Francis Lieber"? And the pen name "Christian Herrmann" once more! In the same line with "Francis Lieber"! Why did not "Francis Lieber" send copy in the "portfolio Columbia" to the nonexistent Kantian Society in Boston instead of painfully recopying the "original"? And why after completing his literary adventure in November, 1865, did "Francis Lieber" postpone sending his literary gem to Boston until April of the next year?

After you have given "perfectly natural answers" to these questions, try identifying "Lieber" with Mr. X.

When a philosopher friend some years ago heard that we were becoming interested in the historical problem presented by the "Lieber" essay, he wrote: "I am interested and somewhat amused that you are casting a critical eye on the problem of Mrs. Eddy and Hegel. . . . I would not take the book [the Haushalter volume] seriously . . . Francis Lieber [did not know] much about Hegel. Follen knew a little more, but even he interpreted him as a 'Kantian'!" [65] After reading the "Lieber" document, one must agree that "Lieber" also knew little about Hegel.

7

The Non-Hegelian Character of the Essay

THE selective comments in the preceding chapter upon "The Metaphysical Religion of Hegel" make the essay on Hegel appear like a little homily on Hegel with English and American literary and religious references added. It consists of twelve pages but the observations upon Hegel begin only on page two and practically end on page ten. At the beginning of the essay, the ghost writer was concerned about Kant's "metaphysical Christ" and toward its end he returns to the same point by way of David Friedrich Strauss, "the great Hegelian," permitting "Emerson, Channing, Parker" to reflect "the Hegelian religion in America in their Unitarian views of Christ and atonement!" [1]

"Lieber" does not seem to realize that transcendental idealism, ethical idealism, physical and aesthetic idealism, and logical idealism are not at all identical. The speculative philosophies of religion of Fichte, Schleiermacher, Schelling, von Baader, Krause, and Hegel have never been synthesized. He fails to discriminate between the various kinds of "identity" represented in Fichte, where nature is subordinated to spirit with contempt for nature; in Schelling, where the real and ideal have equal rights; in Hegel, where nature is subordinated to spirit but without contempt for nature. He misses dialectic completely, so all the differences here go by default. And as for *speculative logic*, the Hegelian achievement, as over against "common logic"—where does it emerge in this sermon?

If the Hegelian triangle is logical idealism, identity, and development, then the homiletically and so briefly mentioned points of "The Metaphysical Religion of Hegel"—idea, God, Person, the good and the beautiful, matter, reflection, evil, man, immortality, and Christ impress one as prekindergarten Hegelianism—jottings from a student's notebook.

Several readings of these nine pages do not prepare the student to pass even an elementary course in Hegel. Only a few Hegelian essays are mentioned, and no one can discover from the meager quotations what it is all about. Where are *anderssein, für sich, an sich, aussersich?* Where are *logisierung, sublimated, aufgehoben?* Where are dialectic method, thesis, antithesis, synthesis? Where are *Sittlichkeit,* the religion of measure, the religion of fantasy, the religion of being in self, the religion of light, the religion of pain, the religion of enigma, the religion of sublimity and unity, the religion of beauty and necessity, the religion of purposiveness and understanding, the religion of truth, of freedom, and of spirit? Where are subjective spirit, objective spirit, absolute spirit? The treatises especially referred to in this essay contain almost 4,500 pages of abstruse argument. Hegel himself could not have popularized them in less than 10,000 pages. Whoever the author of "The Metaphysical Religion of Hegel" was, he could have done a better job if he had consulted Schasler's *Hegel: Populaere Gedanken aus einen Werken.*[2]

How the editor of the little essay could describe it as "a deeply thoughtful discussion of Hegelianism," "a remarkable essay," when Hegelian scholars repudiate it as not at all commensurate with Hegelian dialectic is baffling. "Lieber's" remarks on "reflection" are introduced by "few people comprehend what Hegel in his science means by Reflection." If "Lieber" includes himself, we quite agree. He might have started with Genesis 1:26, Wisdom 7:25, Philo, Hebrews 1:3 ff., I Corinthians 11:7, 15:49, Colossians 1:15, 3:10, and at least moved beyond the puerile. Caird's characterization of Hegel was cruelly exaggerated but is also completely out of agreement with the editor's enthusiasm for "The Metaphysical Religion of Hegel." Caird put it: "... the height of audacity in sewing up pure nonsense, a stringing together of senseless and extravagant mazes of words, such as had previously been known only in madhouses, was finally reached in Hegel, and became the instrument of the most barefaced general mystification that has ever taken place, with a result which will appear fabulous to posterity and will remain a monument to German stupidity."[3] Indeed, one might plausibly argue that the Francis Lieber of history is more in agreement with Caird than with Haushalter.

The Haushalter definition of Hegelianism, like "The Metaphysical Religion of Hegal," can tell what that philosophy comprehends without once using the term "dialectic." It is, therefore, worthy of perpetuation:

Hegelianism may be termed a species of the philosophy of Idealism. A satisfying definition of what constitutes Idealism is a difficult achievement. It calls up St. Augustine's pointed observation about the Divine, "If you ask me what it is I cannot tell you, but if you do not ask me, I know." In general, Idealism maintains that the world is a *construct* of Mind, that the only independent Reality of the universe is not dead matter but active Mind differentiated into Ideas. Individual human minds are parts of the Absolute Mind, or God; matter is an expression or method of reflection of the Infinite Mind; Truth consists in agreement of the individual's ideas with Reality or Ideas as they exist in the Absolute Mind of God. This statement does not pretend to conclude the subject...[4]

The description of Hegel's philosophy in the "Lieber" discourse does not appeal to either European or American Hegelians. One of the former, an enthusiastic Dutch-American Hegelian, in a personal letter tells about how Hegel's philosophy was introduced in Holland early in the twentieth century by Professor Bolland of the University of Leyden. In the course of two decades of teaching, he had some six hundred students attending his lectures. About the same time Christian Science also became well known in the Netherlands. *Yet it never occurred to Bolland to call any attention to similarities between Hegel and Christian Science.*[5]

In another letter, the same student of Hegel thus describes his system:

Hegel is the philosopher of the dialectic method of reasoning. The dialectic method is the result of a critical study of reasoning unfolded in Hegel's phenomenology. It gave Hegel's logic the very complicated structure in which his sentences were written. This complexity was unavoidable since the philosophy deals with categories and not with isolated facts. Those categories had to be discussed completely to show their connections with the philosophical totality. In the dialectic, all philosophical statements show two opposite viewpoints, a positive and a negative and it is only by this drastic method, that in Hegel's philosophy the thought moves from one category to another. It is, therefore, an error to expect to say something against any of his philosophical statements which is not said in the philosophy itself. If, therefore, anybody tries to concentrate attention upon some one statement of Hegel, he gives attention to only half of what Hegel said. *Hegel's philosophy shows that every Hegelian statement has only relative value....*[6]

Hegel's philosophy is essentially phenomenological. The logic results from this. The logic applied to the different areas of human experiences results in the different philosophies.

Each philosophy has two aspects of interpretation: one supports each statement in the philosophy, the other destroys it. *This is the characteristic of Hegel's dialectic.* We get interested in both sides: one, which tends to let us sojourn at a nice spot in his philosophy; the other which urges us to move on...

This enabled the Nazis to misuse Hegel for their own objectives. They have shown a complete ignorance of Hegel's Phenomenology and Logic.[7]

In some further correspondence, this same lifelong student of Hegel wrote:

Hegel's philosophy is an *empirical* doctrine of categories which consists of a *dialectic* treatment of Pure Reason and its Reality, free from any anxious belief or assumption. It can be verified by our experiences. It contains the same categorical relations which in its highest religious form we find in the pictorial presentations of Christianity. For instance, the relation between Pure Reason and Reality is identical with what we call in religion the relation between God and his creation. In religion we *believe* in God; in Hegel's philosophy *the God-concept is unavoidable...*

Without the dialectic, Hegel's philosophy is merely an accumulation of classified ideas. *Without the dialectic, Hegel's philosophy is dead.*[8]

Finally, this brilliant student of Hegel noted the absence of the dialectic in "Lieber's" essay and Haushalter's interpretation alike. "Hegel's philosophy unifies synthetically the categories of beauty, religion and wisdom as a relation of potentiality, reality and idealism, which is a *dynamic* aspect of the dialectic. *It is quite possible that Haushalter and Lieber understand Hegel, but they give no evidence of it*" in *Mrs. Eddy Purloins from Hegel.*[9]

73

A well-known American professor of philosophy wrote to me:

Christian Science is *not* based on Hegel's philosophy, which in fact is incompatible with its teachings.

Royce's chapter on "Optimism, Pessimism, and the Moral Order" in his *The Spirit of Modern Philosophy* gives a clear exposition of the positive interpretation of the problem of evil in Absolute Idealism. His position is essentially that of Hegel. . . . Without real evil there would be no real moral conflict, *no dialectical struggle of opposites and so on.*[10]

Another quite competent student of American idealism has observed that his "survey of New England Idealism has led him to believe that there was practically no understanding of Hegel in New England until Harris came to Concord from St. Louis with the exception of Hedge who had read a little first hand." [11] But Harris was in Concord in the 1880s.

And, again, he writes that "the pages of Haushalter do not report a Hegelian doctrine. Christian Science is influenced by German idealism *only very indirectly through the New England transcendentalism.*" [12]

Professor Royce thinks that Hegel transformed the views of Kant. Hegel drops "accessible" from Kant's "the accessible world is the world as the rational nature of the human Self requires us to interpret it." For Hegel reason is valid only when concerned with the whole. For Kant's phenomena, Hegel has absolute truth. Kant insists upon the reality of ethical ideals, Hegel upon knowledge of truth. For Kant all knowledge is relative, while for Hegel absolute knowledge is possible.

Royce emphasizes the significance of the dialectical movement of Hegel's thinking. Contradiction and negation are at the very heart of Hegel's system. "The denial, or sublation, of the imperfect stages of insight is the only means whereby the perfect stages can be made explicit. This is the principle of the dialectical method." [13]

Kroner also emphasizes the centrality of dialectic in the Hegelian system. Here reason and revelation are dialectically reconciled. His Christianity is spelled out in dialectic. "The victory of truth over reflective intellect can be achieved only as a resurrection. The way leads through the death of separation and returns to the life of primordial identity." [14]

74

Had the author of "The Metaphysical Religion of Hegel" not based his essay upon "his own translations from *Die Philosophie der Religion, Aesthetik, Wissenschaft der Logik*, and *Philosophie der Geschichte*," his interpretation of Hegel might have revealed some knowledge of Hegel's earlier and later systems. In summary, the story is this:

In 1915 Hans Ehrenberg and Herbert Link published an Hegelian manuscript written about 1801-1802, not published prior to Hegel's death and containing an earlier form of the later Logic—the basic principles of knowledge, thought, being, and existence: "this logic deviates from all former conceptions and schemes of logic: it moves. Thought is made mobile." [15] Thinking here means discriminating and opposing and unifying and synthesizing as well. There are four Logics: the Logic of Spirit, in which the separating and objectifying mind is a phase of the reuniting and resubjectifying spirit; the speculative Logic of reason; the Logic of intuition underlying "self as thinking and as thought" and unifying them; and the Logic of being, existence, and reality. Hence, dialectic is the "dialogue of mind with itself." Here is Hegel's fundamental insight, namely, that *Geist* is the "inseparable connection between mind and spirit, between the human and the divine," so that Hegel's metaphysical logic "concerns not only the categories and principles of human knowledge but the forms and categories of Being itself." [16]

In his chapter on Absolute Mind, Hegel (1801) unifies "the theoretical ego and the practical ego"—the former knows itself now as the "Supreme Being" and the "circle of reflection" is closed.

By 1806, Hegel had found his central truth and thenceforward to 1831 was perfecting his system. The inherent, necessary dialectical movement now fused logic and metaphysics. "Thinking always means distinguishing and reuniting the distinguished terms, self-alienation and self-reconciliation. This process is the primordial logical phenomenon. It is also the inner metaphysical nature of the Absolute, the core of mind and spirit." [17]

Contraries are the same; opposites are identical; they belong to the same type or kind as day and night. When the opposition is absolute, the union must be absolute as in case of being and nothing.

In the *Encyclopedia of the Philosophical Sciences*, Hegel relates the history of the Absolute which is Spirit. Spirit is "reason estranged from itself as Nature and returning from this self-estrangement to itself." The Absolute Idea is God before the creation, that is, not the Father of Jesus and of man but the Logos and nothing but Logos. "*In the beginning was the Logos and the Logos was God*"—but only in the beginning. At the end God is the "Father, Son, and Holy Spirit." [18]

The *necessary* movement of the mind in Hegelian dialectic in the 1820s involves movement from subjective (individual) mind to objective (universal) mind to absolute mind realizing itself in art, religion, and philosophy, in right will, willing the right, and so on.

In Hegel's *Philosophy of Right*, according to some critics, the conception of the state was primarily responsible for all the evil deeds of the Prussian kings and their governments, and the brutality and insane cruelty of the Nazis was the logical outcome of the opinions there advocated." [19]

In "The Metaphysical Religion of Hegel," the word "dialectic" is met with once and that single occurrence of this essential Hegelian word sheds no light upon its meaning: "the most difficult point to grasp in the Hegelian *dialectic* is his doctrine of God." [20] This seems to be all "Lieber" knows about "dialectic."

Finally, to settle the question as to whether the Hegel of history is identical with the "Hegel" of "The Metaphysical Religion of Hegel" by "Lieber," Richard Falckenberg's classical description of the Hegelian philosophy is here analyzed. [21]

The philosophy of Hegel, says Falckenberg, is an *intellectualist* view of the world. All being is *realized thought*, all becoming is the *development of thought*. Hence, the *primacy* of *the practical reason* must be discarded and theory as the ground, center, and aim of all existence including the human must be exalted. This results in the three elements of Hegel's system of philosophy: (1) idealism; (2) a system of identity; (3) an optimistic construction of development.

Hegel's idealism is a logical type; it has both a physical and an aesthetic character; "the *concept* is both the subject and the goal of the development." [22]

Hegel's "identity" considers nature and spirit to be one in essence and "phenomenal modes of an absolute" above both nature and spirit. Nature is subordinate to spirit but not a mere instrument for it. It is a transition stage in the development of the Absolute, that is to say, it is "the idea in its *Anderssein*, or "other being." Nature is spirit itself, which becomes nature in order to become actual, conscious spirit. Spirit in itself (*an sich*), the idea of reason, the absolute, becomes nature. "The concept develops from 'in itself' to 'out of self' into 'for-itself.' " From *An-sich* through *Ausser-sich* into *Fuer-sich*—that is the progression of *concept*. The absolute, or concept, exists in three forms: (1) reason (system of logical concepts); (2) nature; (3) living, actual, conscious spirit. Hegel's system of identity subordinates nature to spirit and regards the absolute as a "realm of eternal thoughts," as the ideal.[23]

In his philosophy of development, Hegel is obstinately logical in carrying out the rhythm of thesis, antithesis, and synthesis—his dialectic method. Philosophy is metaphysics, "the science of the absolute and its immanence in the world, the doctrine of the identity of opposites, of the *per se* of things and not merely of their phenomenon."[24] Philosophy must be science from concepts—"only not from abstract concepts." *His concrete concept seeks the universal in the particular.* A concrete concept discovers the infinite in the finite, the absolute in the world, the essence in the phenomenon. "The concrete concept secures the identity of opposites through self-mediation, their passing over into it; it teaches us to know the identity as the result of a process. First, immediate unity, the divergence of opposites, and, finally, the reconciliation of opposites—this is the universal law of all development."[25]

"The transition from being into nothing, and from nothing into being is becoming." A growing boy is both a youth and not a youth![26]

"Reason as the faculty of concrete concepts" is the organ of true philosophy. "The absolute is a process and all that is real is the manifestation of this process." "Philosophy is dialectic, that is, the movement of thought, a system of concepts, each of which passes over into its successor, gives birth to its successor, just as it was born by its predecessor."[27]

Contradiction is the motive power of development. Hence the synthesis is the beginning of a new thesis. The always defective concept is supplemented by its contrary which thereupon becomes a higher but not ultimate concept. Even the absolute idea is not the full, the whole truth. This is the law of advance: (1) Position; (2) to opposition; (3) to new combination, or enriched idea.[28] The Idea becomes Nature which becomes Spirit.

77

Hence, the philosophical system of Hegel is *speculative logic*, philosophy of nature, the doctrine of the subjective spirit, the doctrine of the objective spirit and their unity in the absolute spirit.[29]

Hegel's speculative logic is ontological and metaphysical, consisting of being, essence, and concept. Under being he enlarges upon quality, quantity, and qualitative quantum (the combination of quality and quantity); under essence, he discusses appearance and actuality, which comprehends substantiality, causality, and reciprocity; under concept, subjectivity, objectivity, and Idea.

Subjectivity he breaks down into concept, judgment, syllogism; objectivity, into mechanism, chemism, teleology; Idea, into life, cognition, and Absolute Idea.

The philosophy of nature shows the Idea externalizing itself in order to become actual. But this actuality of nature is of course imperfect and only the precondition to the movement onward toward the actuality of spirit, or *the enriched original idea.*[30]

Freedom, that is, being with or in self, is the essence and destination of subjective spirit. Races, nations, sex, age, sleep, waking hours —anything associated with union of soul and body come under review. The movement is from consciousness to self-consciousness to reason, their synthesis.[31]

The doctrine of objective spirit comprehends right, ethics, social morality.

In right, will attains outer actuality in property, contract, punishment.

In ethics, will attains inner actuality in purpose, intention, welfare, good, evil. But there is conflict between one's intention (the moral law) and one's action (the individual will). Conscience is not secure against error. What is objectively evil may seem good and a duty to the conscience.

In social morality, will attains both outer and inner actuality, that is, complete or perfect actuality. Social morality is *Sittlichkeit* involving family, civil society, and the state which is the completed actualization of the freedom represented in the unity of family and civil society. The perfect form of the state is constitutional monarchy.[32]

In the Absolute Spirit, the subjective spirit and the objective spirit form their synthesis, arrive at unity and spirit, and are at last perfectly free and reconciled. But this reconciliation of the infinite in the finite appears in three forms: (1) As intuition in art and aesthetics; (2) as feeling, representation, symbolism in religion; (3) as thought in philosophy.[33]

The art of the Orient, including the Egyptian and Hebrew, was sublime and symbolic; Greek art was classical and dissolved in Roman satire; the Christian art (painting, music, poety) was romantic, emphasizing love, loyalty, honor, grief, repentance dissolved in humor.

Religion and philosophy differ only in form. The former appears in several forms. Natural religion develops measure among the Chinese, fantasy in Hinduism, being-in-self in Buddhism. The religion of spiritual individuality is represented by the sublimity and unity of Judaism; by the beauty, necessity, wisdom, and bravery of the Greeks; by the severity and world dominion of the Romans.

The religion of spiritual individuality was preceded by transitional forms such as Zoroastrianism, the religion of light; the Syrian religion of pain; the Egyptian religion of mystery and enigma.[34]

It was followed by "the Christian or revealed religion of truth, freedom, Spirit, the unity of the divine and the human."

Philosophy clothes "the absolute content given in religion in the form adequate to it, that is, in concept. In philosophy, the absolute spirit attains the highest stage, its perfect self-knowledge. It is the self-thinking Idea." [35]

Verily, "The Metaphysical Religion of Hegel" and the philosophy of Hegel are incommensurable.

8

The Non-Christian Science Character
of the Essay

THE main contention of the Haushalter interpretation of the "Lieber" documents is that *Science and Health* was derived from Hegelian philosophy. German idealism is the principal background of the Christian Science system and the "Lieber" essay is its immediate and literally used source.[1] Twenty-five per cent of the text of the book is devoted to the demonstration of this claim, with additional minor dicta to the same effect. For example:

The Lieber manuscript gains distinction as one of the most notable documents in the history of American Letters; for Lieber's summation of Hegel's philosophy became none other than the basis of Science and Health.[2]

... her entire teaching on the doctrine of reflection ... was developed from her own conception or misconception of Hegel's philosophy as briefly presented by Francis Lieber.[3]

... Eddyism is Hegelianism point for point.[4]

Many beautiful pages are to be found in *Science and Health* lending rapt expression to the transcendant Idealism of the Hegelian School.[5]

In his *American Thought from Puritanism to Pragmatism*, [Woodbridge] Riley declared the intelligible parts of Science and Health to be Hegelianism.[6]

American orthodoxy in earlier days was accustomed to attack and ridicule the claims of new religious bodies in the United States by charges of dependence for or even plagiarism from their documents. The historical study of the dependence of later Old Testament and New Testament writings upon earlier compositions as well as the extensive use by contemporary preachers of sermons in religious magazines has tended to silence such accusations to some extent.

The books of the New Testament, with only a few exceptions, frequently quote from the Old Testament without mentioning the particular author. Indeed, the first Bible of the Christian Church was the Jewish holy collection. Here more than thirty-nine books were borrowed or appropriated by Christianity without compensation. And often the original context was altered and applied to Christian needs. The fifty-third chapter of Isaiah, for example, is not predictive. Its tenses are past and the servant is Israel. Christian writers made it a prophecy of the death of Jesus. Medieval Christians by allegorization appropriated the Jewish Bible. But when have they accused themselves of plagiarism? In II Timothy 3:16, it is written: "All Scripture is given by inspiration of God." For the ninety-eight per cent of Christians believing this, all sense of individual authorship and therefore of the possibility of any plagiarism with reference to the entire Bible has been canceled.

Consult the Moffatt translation of the Holy Bible, which italicizes New Testament quotations from the Old Testament, and amazement grows over their number. Acts 7 is a mosaic of Old Testament materials. Its compiler dips into a dozen Old Testament books, such as Genesis, Exodus, Isaiah, the Psalter, Daniel, Joshua, Ezekiel, II Samuel, Nehemiah, Leviticus, II Kings, and so on. Are sources mentioned in Hebrews for its numerous direct quotations from the Hebrew Holy Book?

In Mark 1:3, *Matthew* 3:3, *and Luke* 3:4 *the same quotation from Isaiah* 40:3 *is found.* It is made to apply to Jesus by altering the Old Testament "our God" to "him."

Similarly, I Corinthians 14:20-22 does not hesitate to reinterpret Isaiah 28:11 ff., while I Corinthians 15:45 adds "Adam" and "the last Adam a life-giving Spirit" to Genesis 2:7 to obtain the new faith.

A good way to appreciate how absurd it is to accuse New Testament authors of literary piracy is to compare Matthew 3:7-10 with Luke 3:7-9 from "you brood of vipers" to "thrown into the fire" where the identity of words comes to 98.6 per cent. But did Matthew "pirate" from Luke, Luke from Matthew, or both from a common oral or written source?

In Mark 2:23-28 there are 132 words; in Matthew 12:1-8, 165 words; in Luke 6:1-5, 110 words. There are agreements in words, in quotations from the Old Testament, in the Son of Man is Lord of the Sabbath. What are the plagiaristic possibilities as the historian begins his analysis? Mark might have been the source of Matthew and Luke. All three might have used an unknown source. Luke might have taken some verses from Mark and some from another source, and so on. The mere fact of verbal identity does not solve all the probems of literary dependence. Later Christian tradition assigns names to the Gospels. Nowhere in Matthew is Matthean authorship claimed. Nowhere in Mark is Marcan authorship claimed. Nowhere in Luke is Lucan authorship claimed. John 21:24 only states that "this was the disciple whom Jesus loved." About all that is known about authorship of the Fourth Gospel is that it was not written by the son of Zebedee.

It is crystal clear that every existing Gospel was understood to be the property of the Christian brotherhood especially if it cared to accept it as canonical, and for a time there was much liberty in the way the Gospels were quoted so that traces of the Gospel in the *Apostolic Fathers* are often uncertain.[7] Theories of verbal inspiration were constructed only after four Gospels had been selected by the churches from a much longer list in use in the second century and defined as canonical, authoritative, final for faith and practice. The first generation of Christians had no New Testament. For them *the word of the Lord* was controlling. "Jesus saith unto him, I am the way, the truth, and the life"; "the words that I speak unto you, I speak not of myself: but the Father that dwelleth in me, he doeth the works"; "if a man love me, he will keep my words."[8]

Was Jesus of Nazareth original or did he draw upon the tradition of his people, sometimes quoting verbatim from the larger inherited Jewish Bible?

When asked one day what the primary commandment was, the Nazarene replied, "Hear, O Israel; The Lord our God is one Lord: and thou shalt love the Lord thy God with all thy heart, and with all thy soul, and with all thy mind, and with all thy strength: this is the first commandment. And the second is like, namely this, Thou shalt love thy neighbor as thyself. There is none other commandment greater than these."[9] Deuteronomy 6 and Leviticus

19 are here literally quoted. The originality consists in joining them together and even their combination may be due to the worship in the synagogue.[10]

Similarly, Israel had called God "Father" long before the "Our Father" was recited:

And I will be their Father and they shall be my people
He is our Father
O Yahweh, Father and God of my life
Thy Providence, O Father, guides it along.

So few are the passages in the synoptic Gospels ascribing the use of the "Father" title to Jesus that Christian students of the Scriptures become bewildered on discovering the fact, exclaiming, "What, even the concept of God as Father inherited from Judaism!"

Critical analyses of the "Sermon on the Mount" manifest many similarities and identities with the Jewish thought of the time.[11]

The beautiful, inimitable parables of Jesus, while demonstrating his religious and literary originality, have so many parallels in the sayings of the rabbis that most of them by concordance-method could be made dependent.[12]

The dependence of the Lord's Prayer upon Jewish sources is admitted by such conservative Christian scholars as Zahn, who states that it is an "error to regard *Our Father* as a specifically Christian prayer," while others go on to say that "this entire prayer contains Hebrew forms" and it is a prayer "which even today any Jew could recite." Its background is especially the Quaddish, the Shemone 'Esreh, and certain morning and evening prayers of Judaism:

Let His great Name be extolled and hallowed throughout the universe
    which he created according to his will
May his Kingdom be established in your lifetime and your days
May your prayer be accepted by your Father...
Forgive us our sins...
Do not lead us into temptation...[13]

The thinking of Jesus never "went outside of Israelitish, not to say Jewish, patterns of thought." He resolved the Lord and the Prophets "in terms of human conduct." "Therefore you must always treat other people as you would like to have them treat you, for this sums up the Law and the Prophets." This was his distinctive thought, the treatment of one's fellow man in a neighborly way. "The crux of the matter depended on man's neighborly treatment of his fellowman, on his learning to see that the highest self-interests of the individual are only truly served by his treating others as though their interests were his very own, and on making this the test of having accepted an ethical God." [14]

Jude and II Peter are among the twenty-seven writings composing the New Testament. The verbal identities between the two documents are numerous. Is either a literary "pirate" with reference to the other? Do both add distinctive emphases to their materials taken over from the faith of the Christian fellowship?

Jude claims to have been written by "Jude, the servant of Jesus Christ and brother of James," while II Peter begins, "Simon Peter, a servant and an apostle of Jesus Christ," although Peter was dead before A.D. 68 and II Peter was written about mid-second century. Historical criticism would have to add several sentences regarding the ethical standards of the fourth-century Christian churches which finally placed these "epistles" in the New Testament canon. With that problem we are not concerned.

These two epistles were according to the orthodox interpretation inspired by the Holy Spirit and are inerrant. Then verbal identity was not man-made but God-breathed. The King James Version records a dozen agreements between the twenty-five verses of Jude and the chapters of II Peter. When the historian approached the problem of dependence, the conciseness and the vigor of Jude inclined him to accept its greater degree of originality. But whether II Peter borrowed from the New Testament Jude or from some ancestor of both still remains dubious until further research is conducted. Both Jude's and II Peter's text and context would require prolonged study before the matter could finally be settled.

The crux of the matter is here. Both writers believed they were transmitting the core of the common faith of the church. There was no sense of guilt for dependence upon common tradition. Each added his own materials. And the doxology of Jude 25 is pronounced over and over again in the contemporary worship services of the over four hundred kinds of Christian bodies in the United

States without the slightest indication of the presence of quotation marks in the voice or gestures of the clergyman.

The Revelation of John is surcharged with inherited apocalyptic tradition from Jewish and non-Jewish sources, recent and from the dim past. The only originality is the author's particular pattern and application of the myths he is so profusely borrowing. Yet the descriptions of marvelous beauty are his own, and he has no sense of copyright laws preventing him from selecting from the library of apocalyptic deposits available to him. "And I saw a new heaven and a new earth: for the first heaven and the first earth were passed away; and there was no more sea. And I John saw the holy city, new Jerusalem, coming down from God out of heaven ... And I saw no temple therein." [15] "Two very startling things arrest our attention in John's version of the future. The first is that the likest thing to heaven he could think of was a City; the second, that there was no Church in that City"—city "the antipodes of heaven"; no church, the "defiance of all religion." [16]

Some years ago the vocabulary of the New Testament was regarded as unique, one-tenth of its vocabulary being coined by its authors under inspiration.

Some of these distinctive words were gospel, anathema, *epiousios*.[17] But *evangelion* [gospel] was found in the inscription of Priene cut before the birth of Jesus—the birthday of the God has led the world to *"the messages of joy."* *Anathema* is the closing protective charm of the ancient Graeco-Roman curse tablets. And *epiousios*, that puzzling word of the Lord's Prayer, has been found in the Greek papyri.

How the catechisms and translations wrestled with *epiousios!* The Longer Catechism of the Eastern Church renders it: "Give us daily our bread for subsistence," with which the twentieth-century translation is in agreement: "Give us today the bread that we shall need." The Confraternity Version of American Roman Catholicism revises the Douay: "Give us this day our supersubstantial bread" to read "Give us this day our daily bread." Moffatt has: "Give us today our bread for the morrow," while Goodspeed reads: "Give us today bread for the day." The American Revised Version found it difficult to make up its mind, and the Revised Standard Version has two renderings.

Over one-half century ago, in 1889, a papyrus was published

containing *epiousios, with secular significance.* In 1915 a lexicon of words found in Greek papyri mentioned it. But it was 1925 before DeBrunner and Martin Dibelius *independently* noticed this reference. It is found in a memorandum of expenses for ordinary things like straw, peas, etc., and Preisigke translates: *für den Tagesbedarf hinreichend.* Deissmann had long contended that the word came from the *secular* and not the *religious* vocabulary, and his guess was now confirmed.

If the former "unique" vocabulary of the New Testament has now been reduced from 500 words to less than a score and the inspired writers are now found to be using the ordinary vocabulary of the Graeco-Roman world of their day, does that destroy their religious originality? Or was Adolf von Harnack nearer the truth when he judged that Roman, Greek, Jew, and Christian were drawing upon the common reservoir of general aspiration, longing, hope, and sublime thought of the imperial age when they spoke of "the soul, God, knowledge, expiation, asceticism, redemption, eternal life with individualism substituted for nationality." [18]

In the same way, the originality of religious leaders can no longer be disposed of by underlining identities between their thinking and earlier thinking.

Consider the experience of the Founder of Christian Science.

From 1844, at least, Mrs. Eddy was convinced "that God in Christ had a message for the body as well as the soul." [19]

In 1853, she and her husband were conducting the first experiments in the area of her new faith. [20]

Thereupon, Quimby entered the situation, but in 1864 admitted that "Mrs. Eddy had discovered something different from anything *he* had ever taught."

Mr. H. A. L. Fisher in his *Our New Religion* adds a note, stating that this "is on the whole sustained by a study of the Quimby manuscripts published in 1921" and later writes: "If *Science and Health* would never have been written without Quimby, Quimby certainly would never have written *Science and Health;* and in the development of Christian Science that book, and that book only, has been of decisive importance." And Mr. Fisher is writing as a critical historian. [21]

On February 1, 1866, Mrs. Eddy fell upon the ice in Lynn, Massachusetts, and had her call. Her thinking was different from that of Quimby, as George Quimby himself admitted: "The religion she teaches is certainly hers." [22] Notes in Mrs. Eddy's handwriting which Hiram S. Crafts preserved still exist as proof that Mrs. Eddy was already thinking independently of Quimby and identifying the whole idea of man with "the perfect man of God's creating" in 1866 and 1867.[23]

The most striking and important difference between Christian Science and Hegelianism, European students of the problem claim, is the former's emphasis on *the primacy of life*.

But Hegel, says Falckenberg, discards "the primacy of the practical reason; *theory is extolled as the ground, center, and aim of human, nay of all existence*." [24] Christian Science, on the contrary, undertakes *seriously to realize philosophy*. "Between Emerson and Mrs. Eddy there was a great gulf fixed. He was all for thought, and she for demonstration," and precisely here is also the distinction between Hegel and Mrs. Eddy.[25] As Victor Weiss has so clearly seen: "In Christian Science, *idealism does something for life*. Christian Science is genuinely American, fearless, active, youthful. Its challenge is to become doers of the Word, James 1:22. Salvation is not merely from sin as in orthodox Christianity but from disease and death." [26]

"Contrary to common misapprehension, Christian Science does not ignore what it regards as unreal. This religion teaches its adherents to forsake and overcome every form of error or evil on the basis of its unreality; that is, by demonstrating the true idea of reality. This it teaches them to do by means of spiritual law and spiritual power."

"Mrs. Eddy recalled Christianity to its original emphasis, summoned humanity to appreciate that man is the true image of God. When man acknowledges his real being, he becomes one with God." [27] So Mahr, another German scholar of Giessen, concludes.

"Christian Science has elements of mysticism, rationalism and idealism but they are built into the primacy of life. Christian Science originated not out of longing for pure knowledge but because of the desire to master the naturally conditioned life and its needs." [28]

Karl Holl, the eminent German church historian, who penned the best analysis of the Christian Science interpretation of life, begins it thus: "Christian Science is a point of view based upon experience as well as upon reason." Holl, all German scholars admit, enjoyed an unexcelled reputation in Germany as professor of the History of Christianity. For two decades he served as the second ordentlicher professor of Church History as the colleague of the pre-eminent Adolf von Harnack at the University of Berlin, was a member of the Prussian Academy of Sciences there, and produced scores of masterpieces in Church History from the reconstruction of the story of the Apostles' Creed, Epiphanius, monasticism, church festivals to Chalmers of England and Tolstoi (learning Russian to do his subject justice). Between 1903 and 1922 he wrote nine separate monographs on Martin Luther—his greatest contribution to the modern reinterpretation of the great reformer. Three heavy tomes were required for the publication of his scores of monographs. He did only reliable, independent, impartial, creative research. He was not conditioned by ecclesiastical politics and reduced his life span by devotion to his painstaking studies.

His monograph on Christian Science was written in 1917 and ranks with Victor Weiss's *Die Heilslehre der Christian Science* (1927) as one of the two most brilliant primary studies in the German language of this American religious movement.[29]

The following summary based on Holl's analysis of Christian Science seeks to give his findings by quoting alternately from Holl and the source passages in *Science and Health* on which he bases his comment, thus enabling the reader to follow Holl's thought without turning each time to the textbook to discover the basis of his conclusions: [30]

Science and Health: "The time for thinkers has come. Truth, independent of doctrines and time-honored systems, knocks at the portal of humanity. Contentment with the past and the cold conventionality of materialism are crumbling away. Ignorance of God is no longer the stepping-stone to faith. The only guarantee of obedience is a right apprehension of Him whom to know aright is Life eternal. Though empires fall, 'the Lord shall reign forever.'" (Preface vii: 13-21). "Faith, if it be mere belief, is as a pendulum swinging between nothing and something, having no fixity. Faith, advanced to spiritual understanding, is the evidence gained from Spirit, which rebukes sin of every kind and establishes the claims of God. One kind of faith trusts one's welfare to others. Another kind of faith understands divine Love and how to work out one's 'own salvation, with fear and trembling.' 'Lord, I believe; help thou mine unbelief!' expresses the helplessness of a blind faith; whereas the injunction, 'Believe . . . and thou shalt be

88

saved!' demands self-reliant truthworthiness, which includes spiritual understanding and confides all to God." (23:16-20, 23-31)

Holl: "But the possession of this knowledge is also an ethical task. No one makes the transition from belief in error to truth in a single bound."

Science and Health: "The pious Polycarp said: 'I cannot turn at once from good to evil.' Neither do other mortals accomplish the change from error to truth at a single bound." (77:1-4)

". . . but to reach the heights of Christian Science, man must live in obedience to its divine Principle." (Pref., viii: 2-4)

"We apprehend Life in divine Science only as we live above corporeal sense and correct it. Our proportionate admission of the claims of good or of evil determines the harmony of our existence,—our health, our longevity, and our Christianity." (167:6 f.)

Holl: "Cures and healings are not the only important thing in Christianity. Signs merely demonstrate the higher mission of Christ's power."

Science and Health: ". . . . but the mission of Christian Science now, as in the time of its earlier demonstration, is not primarily one of physical healing. Now, as then, signs and wonders are wrought in the metaphysical healing of physical disease; but these signs are only to demonstrate its divine origin,—to attest the reality of the higher mission of the Christ-power to take away the sins of the world." (150:10)

Holl: "In this conflict, man's natural power of will cannot help."

Science and Health: "Human will-power is not Science. Human will belongs to the so-called material senses, and its use is to be condemned. Willing the sick to recover is not the metaphysical practice of Christian Science, but is sheer animal magnetism. Human will-power may infringe the rights of man. It produces evil continually, and is not a factor in the realism of being. Truth, and not corporeal will, is the divine power which says to disease, 'Peace, be still.'" (144:14-22)

"Will-power is capable of all evil. It can never heal the sick, for it is the prayer of the unrighteous; while the exercise of the sentiments—hope, faith, love—is the prayer of the righteous. This prayer, governed by Science instead of the senses, heals the sick." (206:10 ff.) "Christian Science silences human will, quiets fear with Truth and Love, and illustrates the unlabored motion of the divine energy in healing the sick. Self-seeking, envy, passion, pride, hatred, and revenge are cast out by the divine Mind which heals disease. The human will which maketh and worketh a lie, hiding the divine Principle of harmony, is destructive to health, and is the cause of disease rather than its cure." (445:19 ff.)

89

Holl: "*The true method of cure is thus from above down. Man must come to understand who God truly is and what being really is.*"

Science and Health: "Befogged in error (the error of believing that matter can be intelligent for good or evil), we can catch clear glimpses of God only as the mists disperse, or as they melt into such thinness that we perceive the divine image in some word or deed which indicates the true idea,—the supremacy and reality of good, the nothingness and unreality of evil." (205:15 ff.)

Holl: "*When man experiences God as Spirit, he acknowledges his oneness with God, his eternal unity with God. Hence, he is forthwith cured of his selfishness. Selfishness originates with the assumption of many ruling spirits. As soon as man realizes there is only one Spirit, he experiences a sense of unity with all his brethren.*"

Science and Health: "When we realize that there is one Mind, the divine law of loving our neighbor as ourselves is unfolded; whereas a belief in many ruling minds hinders man's normal drift towards the one Mind, one God, and leads human thought into opposite chanels where selfishness reigns." (205:22 ff.)

Holl: "*When this illumination has come, one must adhere to the emphasis upon the Spirit.*"

Science and Health: "Look away from the body into Truth and Love, the principle of all happiness, harmony, and immortality. Hold thought steadfastly to the enduring, the good, and the true, and you will bring these into your experience proportionably to their occupancy of your thoughts." (261:2-7)

Holl: "*It is man's duty to rid himself of all error regarding corporeality, sin, sickness, death, by watchfulness and prayer.*"

Science and Health: "To ascertain our progress, we must learn where our affections are placed and whom we acknowledge and obey as God. If divine Love is becoming nearer, dearer, and more real to us, matter is then submitting to Spirit. The objects we pursue and the spirit we manifest reveal our standpoint, and show what we are winning." (239:16 ff.)

Holl: "*Thus Man bears the cross of Christ.*"

Science and Health: "We must close the lips and silence the material senses. In the quiet sanctuary of earnest longings, we must deny sin and plead God's allness. We must resolve to take up the cross, and go forth with honest hearts to work and watch for wisdom, Truth, and Love. We must 'pray without ceasing.' Such prayer is answered in so far as we put our desires into practice. The Master's injunction is, that we pray in secret and let our lives attest our sincerity." (15:15 ff.)

"...but this can be done only by taking up the cross and following Christ in the daily life." (179:2)

Holl: "The best way to get rid of Error is to pray. Genuine prayer is meditation, silence resting in God. But prayer is not such absorption in God that personality vanishes. Only prayer which issues in corresponding life is genuine. On the mountain top of prayer, evil becomes nothingness and fear vanishes."

Science and Health: "To ascertain our progress, we must learn where our affections are placed and whom we acknowledge and obey as God. If divine Love is becoming nearer, dearer, and more real to us, matter is then submitting to Spirit. The objects we pursue and the spirit we manifest reveal our standpoint, and show what we are winning." (239:16 ff.)

"Audible prayer can never do the works of spiritual understanding, which regenerates; but silent prayer, watchfulness, and devout obedience enable us to follow Jesus' example. Long prayers, superstition, and creeds clip the strong pinions of love, and clothe religion in human forms. Whatever materializes worship hinders man's spiritual growth and keeps him from demonstrating his power over error." (4:27 ff.)

"The closet typifies the sanctuary of Spirit, the door of which shuts out sinful sense but lets in Truth, Life, and Love. Closed to error, it is open to Truth, and *vice versa*. The Father in secret is unseen to the physical senses, but He knows all things and rewards according to motives, not according to speech. To enter into the heart of prayer, the door of the erring senses must be closed. Lips must be mute and materialism silent, that man may have audience with Spirit, the divine Principle, Love, which destroys all error." (15:3 ff.)

"Man is not absorbed in Deity, and man cannot lose his individuality, for he reflects eternal Life; nor is he an isolated, solitary idea, for he represents infinite Mind, the sum of all substance." (250:1 ff.)

"The test of all prayer lies in the answer to these questions: Do we love our neighbor better because of this asking? Do we pursue the old selfishness, satisfied with having prayed for something better, though we give no evidence of the sincerity of our requests by living consistently with our prayer? If selfishness has given place to kindness, we shall regard our neighbor unselfishly, and bless them that curse us; but we shall never meet this great duty simply by asking that it may be done. There is a cross to be taken up before we can enjoy the fruition of our hope and faith." (9:5 ff.)

Holl: "We must be practitioners of the good to help the weak."

It is sometimes asked why Mrs. Eddy labeled the European philosophies "miscalled metaphysical systems . . . reeds shaken by the
wind." *The answer accepted by the German interpreters is because
they "failed to improve the conditions of mortals morally, spiritually, or physically,"* for example:

Leibnitz, Descartes, Fichte, Hegel, Spinoza, Bishop Berkeley were
once clothed with a "brief authority" but Berkeley ended his metaphysical theory with a treatise on the healing properties of tar water
and Hegel was an inveterate snuff-taker. The circumlocutions and
cold categories of Kant fail to improve the conditions of mortals,
morally, spiritually, or physically. Such miscalled metaphysical systems are reeds shaken by the wind . . ." [31]

Weiss, therefore, concludes his chapter on the originality of
Christian Science with *"the principle which binds together the
Christian Science system and clarifies its structure, is the primacy
of the natural life."* [32] *This view was alien to Hegel.* The activism
of Christian Science, its reinterpretation and transformation of
idealism into practical values is the major difference between Hegelianism and Christian Science. At most, then, there is only a very
general, indirect, and remote agreement between some aspects of
German idealism and *Science and Health,* as has been acknowledged
since the days of Royce.

With these German historians and philosophers Lyman P. Powell
seems to be in agreement when he writes:

Before Mrs. Eddy's day, metaphysical discussion of the nature of
the universe was mere theorising. It was academic; it smelt of the
lamp. . . . The utmost that even Hegel, most inclusive of all metaphysical idealists, set the idealist doing was to teach the world to understand
itself, *not to reform itself,* according to philosophy. . . .
Not so Mrs. Eddy. She would turn theory into practice. She would
have her followers live up to her philosophy. . . . [33]

Why do Germans acquainted with Christian Science find resem-
blances to *Science and Health* in Fichte rather than Hegel? Because
Hegel was not interested in the primacy of life. This is how
Falckenberg describes Fichte:

The world can be understood only from the standpoint of spirit,
only from the will. The ego is pure activity, and all reality its product.

92

Fichte's system is all life and action: its aim is not to mediate knowledge, but to summon the hearer and reader to the production of a new and pregnant fundamental view, in which the will is as much a participant as the understanding, it begins not with a concept or a proposition, but with a demand for action;... its God is not a completed absolute substance, but a self-realizing world-order.[34]

Even after Fichte went to Berlin, in his second period, he did not substitute "the inactive absolute in place of the active absolute ego, and the quiet blessedness of contemplation in place of ceaseless action. *Not in place of these, but beyond them*, while all else remained as it was." [35]

It was Fichte who produced those "glowing *Addresses to the German Nation*, 1808, which essentially aided in arousing the national spirit and *caused his name to live as one of the greatest of orators and most ardent of patriots in circles of the German people where his philosophical importance cannot be understood.*" [36]

And that is why there is inscribed on his monument: "The teachers shall shine as the brightness of the firmament, and *they that turn many to righteousness as the stars that shine forever and ever.*" [37]

Victor Weiss puts it tersely and decisively when he affirms that "Christian Science is solely and only interested in the possession of knowledge, not in the acquisition of knowledge, and this principally differentiates between Christian Science and all other science." [38]

And Weiss, after calling attention to possible similarities between this and that in Christian Science and the German Idealism, refuses to reject the argument for the *autochthonous* origin of Christian Science. Mrs. Eddy may mention Fichte and Hegel but only to claim the infinite superiority of Christian Science: "Compared with the inspired wisdom and infinite meaning of the Word of Truth, they are as moonbeams to the sun, or as Stygian night to the kindling dawn." [39]

Karl Holl also is not at all in doubt about the originality of Mrs. Eddy.[40]

And how does George Mahr, the author of the comprehensive article on *Christian Science* in the most authoritative of all pre-Hitler religious encyclopedias in Germany, namely, *Religion in Geschichte und Gegenwart*, judge the work of Mrs. Eddy? Mrs.

Eddy, he concludes, seems to have experienced the ideas of Quimby completely independently and to have greatly expanded them.[41]

And Walter M. Haushalter, in spite of himself, gives testimony to the originality of Mrs. Eddy again and again:

To illustrate how Mrs. Eddy weaves the ideas of Hegel *in new combinations.*

It was only to be expected that Mrs. Eddy's appropriation of Hegelianism *would be shaped by the confines of her own peculiar mind,* on the same principle that water dipped from the infinite sea takes the shape of the conveying bucket.

When the Hegelian school pronounced there are no "accidents" or secondary properties in God, *Mrs. Eddy twists it into meaning, "Accidents are unknown to God."*

Hegel is an *Objective Idealist,* making the substance of matter to consist in Ideas. Mrs. Eddy is a *Subjective Idealist, denying the existence of the phenomenal world altogether.*

On the theoretical denial of evil, Mrs. Eddy and Hegel are most nearly at one.

Although Mrs. Eddy in general presents a fictional or mythological interpretation of Christ, bearing considerable likeness to that of Strauss, *this generalization concerning her fails like all others. She cannot definitely be catalogued theologically with the Strauss-Hegelian school because her consistency on the item attains only about seventy-five per cent.*[42]

Recall again how Mrs. Eddy records her experience: "In the year 1866, I discovered the Christ Science or divine laws of Life, Truth, and Love, and named my discovery Christian Science." [43]

Weiss argues that the crisis for Mrs. Eddy came in connection with the death of Quimby. *She had to depend solely upon herself and discovered the healing power she sought in herself. This discovery was her revelation.* Knowing her difference from Quimby, revulsion was inevitable. She became the shaping personality back of Christian Science. She was incorporated in her teachings. The inner comprehension and experience were *her awakening.* She felt herself original and she was.[44] And without *her* faith in *her* revelation, Christian Science cannot be appreciated.

Powell is of the same opinion:

But, as her understanding grew with ripening experience, she was soon filling old words and phrases with new meaning, then coining her own unquestioned terms to elucidate her system, and at last in obedience to the same persistent urge, writing the book. . . . Hers was that real discovery which consists of finding an age-old truth, settling in it, sharing it with others, and making the most of it for the redemption of the world from sickness, sin and death.[45]

And the newer psychology emphatically subscribes to this finding.[46]

The likeness and alleged parallels between Christian Science and other philosophies and religious systems which exist do not make any assumed dependence more than hypothetical and indirect. Its final objective is the spiritualization of all things. If God is truly Love, how can there be sickness or evil? If God is all and is Spirit, how logically can there be matter? Error must be unreal, since it is the negation of truth.

And, finally, recall again what has been insisted upon by Victor Weiss in demonstrating the originality of Mrs. Eddy as over against the German idealism, that it exists in three major differences or emphases: in the spiritualizing of all things: in the replacing of the human consciousness by God so that man becomes the manifestation of God, and that, therefore, Reason can mobilize the power of Mind for human good; and in *the principle of the primacy of life*.[47]

In the atomic age, all interpretations of man and the universe are needed to help overcome confusion. Appreciation and understanding must replace our temptations to disparage other religions than our own. Mrs. Eddy's vindication should promote the brotherhood of man.

Indeed, the great German interpreters of Christian Science declare that its persuasive and attractive power today results from its emphasis upon the practice of the presence of God, originating in the miracle of healing. The longing for health and peace in the contemporary world of degeneration and confusion and instability ties in with its powerful idealistic ethical trend emphasizing selflessness, purity, love, discipleship to Christ, the incorporation of the individual into a living religious brotherhood and into a closed, simplified view of the world with a freer, practical, philosophical attitude toward the Bible and church organization.

From the religio-social point of view, they say, Christian Science is typically American in spirit. "*In ihr aeuszert sich der Ameri-*

canischer religioeser Mensch am reinsten und am typischsten,"
which by interpretation signifies that the purest and most typical
expression of the American religious personality is found in
Christian Science.

Jesus of Nazareth believed that "by their fruits ye shall know
them" and that the only demonstration of the superiority of his
ethics was the superior life of his followers.

Having thus examined the tenets of Christian Science principally
by appeal to authorities upon both Hegel and Christian Science in
the homeland of German idealism, scholars whose study has been
scientific and objective, we conclude with a late appraisal by a
Swiss-American scholar, Henry Steiger, who has written the most
thorough and scientific analysis of Christian Science to date:

Whether Mrs. Eddy was influenced in the formulation of her doctrine by other writers such as Hegel is of little importance, if we
realize that in the introduction of systematic practical metaphysics
Mrs. Eddy was a pioneer.

The two, theory and practice, give the adequate certainty of the
correctness of such a Christ Science.

Mrs. Eddy called her discovery a science and not a philosophy because she started out with facts and not with a theory.

*...the most vital part of Christian Science, its practical application,
is not to be found in Hegel.*

Hegel reaches out for a position which the doctrine of Christian
Science takes consistently.[48]

9

Francis Lieber Did Not Compose the *"Lieber" Essay*

IN connection with the discussion of Lieber's relation to the covering letter, various arguments were offered indicating that Francis Lieber did not compose it, thus raising historical doubts regarding his authorship of the "Lieber" essay. They need not be repeated here.

Possibly a further word regarding the religion of Lieber is called for. Lieber could not have endorsed the religion of Hegel as the "Lieber" essay does so often. This follows from his well-known early religious affirmations. Lieber did not regard his pastor, Pauli, an evangelical minister, preparing him for confirmation, as "sufficiently devout, and I went on for myself in my religious excitement," composing his own psalms and prayers, reading the Bible, instructing his younger brother. He prayed as often as five times an hour and did not overlook prayers "for a war to liberate the fatherland." He joined the *Turners* and shouted for nationalism. He liked Schleiermacher and other "ardently Prussian theologians" for their nationalism. The official songbook of the *Turners* was a "remarkable hodgepodge of 'children's, people's, love, wine, Fatherland, and church songs.'"

After reaching the United States, Lieber's religious views underwent some change and by 1831 he was obliged to defend himself from unfavorable reports by stating that he discussed religious problems only with friends who understood. In South Carolina he objected to the hell-fire and eternal damnation type of preaching, to divines of the "sectarian holiness" brand. He did not accept the "very puerile theory of an inspired origin of language" but his

Presbyterian neighbors dissented. Lieber attended the "Episcopal rather than Thornwell's Presbyterian services—though most often he would stay home: 'For all the sermons I could hear would be either fiery like Chinese dragons or drowsy like stuffed serpents.'" He wrote letters against Catholicism, such as "the Roman Church is a transfer of the Roman Caesarism—stringent despotism—to an empire of religious name of fictitious origin. It is the worst of Absolutisms, incompatible with Liberty—an abject Monarchy, and we Americans will have our sanguinary contest for religious liberty here in our very bowels."

But all this is a far cry from the theology of the "Lieber" document, that is, from left-wing Hegelianism.[1]

The editors of the Haushalter volume[2] insist that "the better part of *Science and Health* was outright Kantian Transcendentalism" and thereupon contend that *Science and Health* is a verbal reproduction of the "Lieber" essay. Since Hegel is not Kant, the contradiction at this point is serious.

The thesis of the Haushalter study that the Lieber of history composed the "Lieber" document cannot be defended on historical considerations.

Freidel, who has written a most critical and dependable biography of Francis Lieber, who above any other American scholar ought to know the style of the Lieber of history, informs the readers of *Francis Lieber, Nineteenth Century Liberal* that the style of the alleged Lieber essay on Hegel is not identifiable with that of the writings and letters of Lieber that he has studied so many years. Lieber's writing style was "frigid, jejune, angular, thorny, and indigestible."[3]

Freidel also examined the photostats of the manuscript on Hegel at Johns Hopkins University Library and concluded that "in many essential ways the handwriting seems to differ from that of Lieber. The hand of the manuscript and of the alleged endorsement by Mary Baker Eddy bear a marked resemblance...," we have noticed.[4]

When the Lieber edition of the *Encyclopedia Americana* of the 1830s is examined to ascertain his interest in the names mentioned in "The Metaphysical Religion of Hegel," another surprise is in store for the student. Remember that even this first American edition consisted of almost seven million words and a total of almost eight thousand pages and that hundreds of articles were added to the *Brockhaus Conversations—Lexikon* of 1812. For Lieber, after a biennium of residence in the United States, this encyclopedia was a grand achievement even with the aid of 24-year-old Wigglesworth (who was so handsomely rewarded for his efforts at translation by 50 cents per German page) and the assistance of his able wife. It was a best seller at $32.50 per set. This first edition of the *Encyclopedia Americana* provided thousands of pages for Lieber to expand a little upon the life of men mentioned in the little twelve-page essay. If he was so interested in all these great men as to use up space in the tiny essay, ought he not to have paid them tribute in the many-volumed encyclopedia? Call the roll of the celebrities mentioned in the essay! Baader, Bluntschli, Coleridge, Channing, Emerson, Follen, Fichte, Feuchtersleben, Hegel, Jesus, Kant, Krause, Leibnitz,[5] Menzel, Orelli, Pope, Parker, Schelling, Strauss. Some of these are not mentioned at all. Hegel gets less than a page; Kant has over six columns; Leibnitz has over eight columns. Jesus is given about a page and the description is not illuminating but simple and commonplace. *He does not discriminate between the Jesus of history and the Christ of faith.* Jesus was executed as a disturber of the public peace. The darkening of the sun at the death of Jesus seems doubtful to Lieber.

All in all, the Lieber of the *Encyclopedia Americana* appears to be a different person from the "Lieber" of the essay on Hegel. Could the inventor of the essay on Hegel have seized upon the name of Lieber as author because Lieber had edited the *Encyclopedia Americana* and that in the very year that the alleged "Kantian Society" was born?

The style and plan of this "Lieber" essay impress the reader as a prayer-meeting homily rather than as the product of an historical mind. It has an introduction, a ten-point exposition of a few ideas in which the preacher was interested, a bric-a-brac discourse on Christianity according to Friedrich Strauss, "wandering into wider and wider variation"; 445 lines are devoted to exposition and 110 lines to connect with stray thoughts appended as notes. Can this be Francis Lieber of General Orders No. 100 fame, "experienced political theorist," "basis for a code of the laws of war drawn up by a congress of scholars . . . leading to the Hague Conventions of 1899 and 1907"?[6]

The points of the essay are:

Point one, 44 lines, explains what Hegel means by idea, a sorry attempt.

Point two, 75 lines, as a definition of "God" fails miserably in elucidating Hegel's concept.

Point three, 45 lines, skims the surface of "person."

Point four, 30 lines, remarks upon "the good, the beautiful, and the true."

Point five, 84 lines, is devoted to "matter."

Point six, 41 lines, does not do anything with "reflection."

Point seven, 45 lines, on "evil" is too general for the auditors to get the drift.

Point eight, 48 lines, on "man" is immediately continued in Point nine, 64 lines, on the "body," where the sermonizer calls upon Kant for first aid in that astounding title, *Von der macht des gemuths den blossen vorsatz seiner Krankhaften gefuglemeister zu sein!* [7] At this stage in the reading of "Lieber's" "profound" treatise, the ghost members of the "Kantian Society, Boston Lyceum" came up the third time for more air.

Point ten dilates upon "Immortality" in 69 lines.

The homilist now leaps from Hegel to Strauss to discuss in 110 lines such matters as Strauss' Christ of faith, the atonement, miracle, allegorization of myth, the Bible, angels, virgin birth, heaven, resurrection, ascension. And with mention of distinguished Americans the preacher subsides into a final quote from Hegel which retracts anything heretical he may have said and adds two footnotes which one at least can comprehend, signing them *Lieber*.

How could a political scientist like the authentic Lieber have failed to dilate upon the "most brilliant and lasting achievement" of Hegel—his view of the development of history and of the state! When one recalls what fifty years ago was still the generally peddled view of history in so many college classrooms and in commencement sermons, it is amazing to have Francis Lieber pass it by in this essay on Hegel. Lieber was "fundamentally practical." In his inaugural address in the South Carolina College he emphasizes the primary importance of history in a democracy. For history is "practical morals." In a republic, history was very significant as governing "the conduct of individuals as 'makers, executors and defenders of the laws and institutions of their society.'" "History is the memory, and on account of careless, guilty ignorance!" [8]

To convince the reader how significant the point is, here is Falckenberg's summary of Hegel's interpretation of history:

His view of the state as the absolute end, the complete realization of the good, is dominated, no doubt, by the antique ideal, which cannot take root again in the humanity of modern times. But his splendid endeavor to "comprehend" history, to bring to light the laws of historical development and the interaction between the different spheres of national life, will remain an example for all time. The leading ideas of his philosophy of history have so rapidly found their way into the general scientific consciousness that the view of history which obtained in the period of the illumination is well nigh incomprehensible to the investigator of today.

History is progress in the consciousness of freedom. At first one only knows himself free, then several, finally all. This gives three chief periods, or rather four world-kingdoms,—Oriental despotism, the Greek (democratic) and the Roman (aristocratic) republic, and the Germanic monarchy,—in which humanity passes through its several ages. Like the sun, history moves from east to west. China and India have not advanced beyond the preliminary stages of the state; the Chinese kingdom is a family state, India a society of classes stiffened into castes. The Persian despotism is the first true state, and this in the form of a conquering military state. In the youth and manhood of humanity the sovereignty of the people replaces the sovereignty of one; but not all have yet the consciousness of freedom, the slaves have no share in the government. The principle of the Greek world, with it fresh life and delight in beauty, is individuality; hence the plurality of small states, in which Sparta is an anticipation of the Roman spirit. The Roman Republic is internally characterized by the constitutional struggle between the patricians and the plebeians, and externally by the policy of world conquest. Out of the repellent relations between the universal and the individual, which oppose one another as the abstract state and abstract personality, the unhappy imperial period develops. In the Roman Empire and Judaism the conditions were given for the appearance of Christianity. This brings with it the idea of humanity: every man is free as man, as a rational being. In the beginning this emancipation was religious; through the Germans it became political as well. The remaining divisions cannot here be detailed. Their captions run: The Elements of the Germanic Spirit (The Migrations; Mohammedanism; the Frankish Empire of Charlemagne); the

Middle Ages (the Feudal System and the Hierarchy; the Crusades; the Transition from Feudal Rule to Monarchy, or the Cities); Modern Times (the Reformation; its Effect on Political Development; Illumination and Revolution).[9]

And all the "Lieber" of the essay has from Hegel's *Philosophy of History* is apparently a few separate slight quotes, such as "The Absolute Spirit is Truth." [10]

A translation with which the inventor of the "Lieber" essay was very pleased follows:

Immanuel Kant expected that this new German metaphysics would create a revolution in the thought of the whole world like that created by Copernicus in the celestial astronomy. "Our position is like that of Copernicus in Astronomy (Kant, *Kritik der reinen Vernunft*), who found it impossible to describe the motions of the heavenly orbs by the idea of their turning about the beholder, wondered if it would not be a truer explanation that the beholder revolves and the heavenly orbs stay at rest. We make a like attempt in metaphysics." (Translated from Hartenstein's edition of the *Kritik*, page 19) [11]

He mentions with joy that he had personally translated it.

It sounds like a preacher's digression and gives the impression that this quote was superlatively important to Kant. The various editions of Hartenstein's *Kant* examined had no such statement on page 19. Finally in Hartenstein, 1867, it was found on page 18. *If the inventor used that edition, there is further proof here that the essay was not written in 1865 or the covering letter in 1866.*

However that may be, one gets the impression that this passage is from the body of the *Kritik der reinen Vernunft*. But it is not. It is from the *Preface to the Second Edition*, 1787, the first edition having been printed in 1781. In the original context there is no such implication as contained here. The observation is just tossed in by Kant as he moves along in his preface.

The word "astronomy" is conspicuous by its absence. There is no hint of either the word or a Copernican book upon the subject in Kant's preface. *The source of it is obviously Science and Health, page 119:25-31.* This is further evidence that *Science and Health* is being employed by the inventor. Moreover, this translation of Kant's German is so slipshod that Lieber could not be charged with it. Again, the inventor translates the last sentence in his quote:

"We make a like attempt in metaphysics." But what Kant wrote was: "A similar experiment can be tried in metaphysics as regards the *intuition* of objects." But the inventor did not know that *Anschauung* is Kant's German for intuition and so made the blunder. But if to all the other mistakes in German in the document we may now add this, what would be the result if a person compared the various quotes in this essay with what Hegel actually wrote?

To enable the reader to see how serious the charge is, we place the quotation in parallel columns with Kant's text and the translation by N. K. Smith in his volume on Kant's *Critique of Pure Reason* (1929), page 22:

The Smith Translation	*Kant's Text*	*"Lieber" Text*
We should then be proceeding precisely in the lines of Copernicus' p r i m a r y hypothesis. Failing of satisfactory progress in explaining the movements of the heavenly bodies on the supposition that all revolved around the spectator, he tried whether he might not have better success if he made the spectator to revolve and the stars to remain at rest. A similar experiment can be tried in metaphysics as regards the intuition of objects.	es ist hiemit eben so, als mit den ersten Gedanken des Copernicus bewandt, der nachdem es mit der Erklaerung der Himmelsbewegungen nicht gut fort wollte, wenn er annahm das ganze Sternheer drehe sich um den Zuschauer, versuchte, ob es nicht besser gelingen moechte, wenn er den Zuschauer sich drehen liess und dagegen die Sterne in Ruhe liess. *In der Metaphysik kann man nun, was d i e Anschauung der Gegenstaende betrifft, es auf* aehnliche Weisse versuchen.	Our position is like that of Copernicus in *A s t r o n o m y* (Kant, *Kritik der reinen Vernunft*), *who found it impossible to describe* the motions of the heavenly orbs by the idea of their turning about t h e beholder, *wondered if it would not be a truer explanation that the beholder* revolves and the heavenly orbs stay at rest. *We make a like attempt in metaphysics.* (Translated f r o m Hartenstein's edition of the *Kritik*, page 19.)

Could a cultured German like Francis Lieber possibly mutilate Kant in this fashion and so transform the original context?

The following paragraph from the "Lieber" document presents difficulties:

Such is the significance of the Hegelian metaphysics of religion. It first came when Christianity most needed it, when bankruptcy by natural science was staring us in the face. Of this critical situation says Strauss, "Kant had pointed out a narrow way through which philosophy might still secure a legitimate store of reliable knowledge; his followers took the path indicated and so far as they kept within it they found themselves rewarded." (*Life of Jesus*) The suggestion of Kant for a metaphysical religion high and safe above the mere historical and dogmatic was fulfilled in the Absolute Religion of Hegel. It is now flowering and even beginning to bear fruit in Germany, promising the full completion of the Reformation begun by Martin Luther. It is entering England and America as well. Spiritual rationality and free thought accompany the new Science of religion and cannot be put down. They will soon supplant the old and emancipate humanity." [12]

No loss in sequence of thought between what precedes and what follows in the essay would be experienced by the reader if this paragraph were omitted.

Observe the quotation marks after the last word: *humanity*. But one looks in vain for the beginning of this quotation. Was it merely a mistake by "Lieber" or is it acknowledgement of dependence upon some book he had been using? In favor of the latter interpretation are these considerations:

Any critical reader of this little twelve-page essay is very puzzled by "Lieber's" frequent reference to Kant, Schelling, and Fichte in addition to Hegel. Kant appears, for example, in 17 references and Fichte in 7, with Schelling a poor third. Moreover, Kant is mentioned before Hegel at the beginning of the essay and after Hegel in the very last "Note" on page 12 of the photostat. Why is Kant so much on the mind of preacher "Lieber"? Why does the paragraph close with the prophecy of the success of the absolute religion of Hegel?

The paragraph is in part obviously borrowed from some book "Lieber" has been quoting from throughout his brochure. Could it be *Science and Health*, page 223:14-24?

"Lieber" document	*Science and Health*
Spiritual rationality and free thought accompany *the new science of religion* and cannot be put down. They will soon supplant *the old* and emancipate humanity.	Spiritual rationality and free thought accompany *approaching Science*, and cannot be put down. They will emancipate humanity, and supplant unscientific and *so-called laws*.

The homily gives the impression of uniting Christian Science views with snatches of ideas from Hegel, Kant, Fichte, Schelling. Were the lectures at Concord sufficient for this or had "Lieber" stumbled upon a book which seemed to combine the four German philosophers for him? Was another of his sources a book on Hegel by Edward Caird, Master of Balliol College, Oxford, whom the Germans refer to as "principal apologist for the new-Hegelianism, who made a deep impression upon English thought, and was a glowing defender of Idealism?"

The original publication of Caird's book on Hegel in the Blackwood philosophical classics for English readers was in 1883 when the Concord Hegelian summer school was going strong. Why should not the original of "Lieber" have been doing collateral reading in Caird?

Caird's Chapter VI has this title: "The Problem of Philosophy—Statement of it by *Kant, Fichte, Schelling,* and *Hegel*." Here is the actual quartette appearing so conspicuously in "Lieber's" essay. With so many others to choose from, why this coincidence?

Take the quotation by "Lieber" about the glorious future of Hegel's philosophy. Whence the optimism? At the moment with the left-wing and right-wing Hegelians locked in mortal combat it looked more like the demise of Hegelianism. According to Caird, Hegelian philosophy seemed to Germany to have "entirely lost the credit which it partially retains in other countries" (page 222).

But then the Scottish philosopher peers deeper into his crystal ball and his discerning eye sees: "For any one whose view is not limited by words or superficial appearances, it is not difficult to see that, in the scientific life of Germany as of other countries, there is no greater power at present than Hegelianism, especially in all that relates to metaphysics and ethics, to the philosophy of history and of religion" (page 223).

That "Lieber" is quoting from *Science and Health* is shown by his use of "*new* science of religion" instead of the "Science" of Mrs. Eddy, since Mrs. Eddy coined the expression "Science and Health" to emphasize the primacy of the practical.

Caird supplies the missing link to explain "Lieber's" "but a few years, Hiram, and you shall see the triumph of German metaphysics all over the world" [13] and "it is now flowering and even beginning to bear fruit in Germany.... It is entering England and

America as well..." [14] Thus *Science and Health*, lectures at the Concord Summer School of Philosophy,[15] and Caird on Hegel are among the sources used by "Lieber" to compose "The Metaphysical Religion of Hegel."

In the findings it will be shown that "Lieber" copied the mistakes of the translator of the celebrated Pfleiderer published in 1887 in regard to "Ormight," invented by Krause. The use of this impossible German without a word of comment indicates that "Lieber" is not the Francis Lieber who died in 1872.

The matter of the use of the pen name "Christian Herrmann" by Francis Lieber in 1865 and 1866 cannot be laughed away by reference to his employment of pseudonyms on other occasions. For he publishes his own name in the same covering letter and essay, one recalls. Moreover, his removal from his professorship in Columbia and protested assignment to a position in the Columbia Law School had been given such publicity that an authorship of the essay on Hegel could not have been long concealed. In June, 1865, President Barnard of Columbia University requested his Board of Trustees to remove Lieber from his professorship. Lieber accused Barnard of "playing university politics to punish him for his Radical Republicanism." The controversy between president and professor was bitter, but Lieber was shifted to the Law School.

Beyond this, Lieber was definitely an egotist. "His audiences regarded him with great respect, but sometimes smiled a bit at his extreme self-assurance." The publisher, George Haven Putnam, recalled how Lieber entered his office one morning and said: "Now, friend Putnam, and you Putnam Jr., who in your opinion is the most conceited man at this time in our country?" The Putnams didn't say but *thought*: Lieber! He could see only communism ahead if a woman were elected president of the United States. "He refused to translate Bluntschli's code of international law into English with the remark that such a profound volume would not sell unless profusely illustrated with female nudes." [16]

The logical absurdity of a brave man and superlative egotist using a pseudonym to conceal his identity from a nonexistent Kantian Society, Boston Lyceum, when the value of his communication to them depended upon their knowing his identity, and then exposing himself by adding his true name is such a hoax as to make a Barnum-Bailey clown hide himself for an entire season for shame.

Lieber's natural attitude is represented in this statement: "Let people assail me publicly; I am ready for any attack but I will not answer back-biters." The Presbyterians he was certain were persecuting him. He himself was on the warpath against Jefferson Davis, Charles Darwin, Thomas Jefferson, feminism, and all the rest to be tempted to hide the publicity he liked under a bushel of pseudonymity. Could the man who wrote regarding the backers of Darwin, they "not only prove to you that your grand-mother was a hideous gorilla, but they do it with enthusiasm and treat you almost like a heretic if you will not agree" and called Thomas Jefferson the "very underminer of the Union—a most mischievous ferret" and dreamed so contentedly about "the mailed fist of Prussian militarism" and lamented that "Hegel had done infinite harm to the cause of science. Instead of earnest, thoughtful investigation, and a discreet acknowledgement of precious experience, he is full of arrogance and presumption," who admired Schleiermacher but disliked Hegel, and this at the very time when "Lieber" accuses Lieber of organizing a Kantian Society, could he have written that eulogy of Hegel found in the essay: "This demonstration of immortality places Hegel in the forefront of the world of thinkers of all time"[17] or this one from the same brochure: "the great Hegel, the flower of German metaphysics"?[18]

Julia Ward Howe's irrefutable testimony in her *Reminiscences* blows away all the fictional dust that has been deposited upon the career of Lieber by the publication in 1936 of the "Lieber" essay.

An item given by Francis Lieber himself to Mrs. Howe follows. In the days of the Napoleonic invasion of Germany Lieber had gone to war with other young men of his university. Recovering from a severe wound, Lieber returned to the lectures in philosophy given by Hegel. That day, before beginning his lecture, Hegel looked the class over and shouted: "Let all those fools who went out against the French depart from this class."[19] Does this exhibition of Hegelian temper account for the genuine Lieber's description of Hegel as a man of weak character?[20]

It was on February 25, 1866, a few weeks before "Lieber" wrote the puzzling covering letter that Mrs. Howe recorded in her diary this memorable statement regarding the Francis Lieber of history: "Rode with Lieber as far as Baltimore. He heard Hegel in his youth and thinks him, as I do, *decidedly inferior to Kant, morally as well as philosophically.*" [21]

Lieber described Hegel as having "done infinite harm to the cause of science. Instead of earnest, thoughtful investigation, and a discreet acknowledgement of previous experience, he is full of arrogance and presumption." [22]

Lieber, likewise, accused Hegel of semantic blunders:

German philosophers, especially Hegel, very frequently found their reasonings upon distinctions arising out of words, and not necessarily, out of different ideas ... They fall, in their own way, into the common error of taking that which in form or name *now* appears to be distinct or *sui generis*, as essentially so, or as having always been so. So the State. So Hegel's *Sein und Werden* ... Suppose Hegel had been an Englishman, in whose language the distinction does not exist ... [23]

Lieber criticized Hegel's historical views:

Even so with institutions, with History. *Gott lebt in der Geschichte.* This is true if properly understood, but it seems that if we first abstract History, than imagine the *Geist der Geschichte* as an independent entity and finally say *Gott ist die Geschichte, as Hegel*, I think, says, and farther consider each historic action or every action, great or small, as only a concrete manifestation of this *Geist*, I cannot see that there is any difference between this and the mentioned case of the Hindoos. [24]

Lieber found fault with Hegel for the turn in German politics in the 1850s.

The shallow German democratic politics are in a measure owing to him; the shallow literature etc. And mark, the former has taken place in spite of Hegel himself, for he wished to be an *absolutist* ... [25]

Early in 1859 a catalogue of books belonging to Lieber was compiled by his wife, Mathilda, and his son, Norman. [26] The authors were arranged alphabetically and the compilation consists of 417 handwritten pages.

The entries for the Classics are found on 5 pages; for Language, on 13 pages; for Religion, on 15 pages; for Literature, on 19 pages; for Law, on 42 pages; for History, on 73 pages; Lessing is represented with *Saemmtliche Werke*; Herder, with 7 works; the Grimms, with 4; and Goethe, with 4.

But the German "idealists" are conspicuous by their absence.

Lieber had only one book by Kant (*Anthropologie*, Leipzig, 1831); one book by Schelling (*Die Lehre von der unvordenklichen zeit*, Munich, 1835); not one book by Fichte; one or two by Hegel (*Philosophy of History*, London, 1857 (translated by I. Sibree), and *Lehre vom Staat* (erased). *There was no book by Strauss.* The "Lieber" essay lets "Lieber" quote frequently from Hegel's *Aesthetik, Logik,* and *Philosophie der Religion;* the Lieber of history had in his library only Hegel's *Philosophy of History* in translation and *Lehre vom Staat* (erased). The "Lieber" essay proudly claims: "The passages quoted in this paper are my own translations from the *Philosophie der Religion, Aesthetik, Wissenschaft der Logik,* and *Philosophie der Geschichte.*" [27] It does take the infinite faith of a grain of mustard seed to believe that Francis Lieber left the privacy of his library, where he had Hegel's *Philosophy of History* in translation, for the Columbia University or the public library to read it in the original German! Lacking that faith, one can only reach the same verdict found sound on so many previous occasions: Francis Lieber may not be identified with the author of the "Lieber" document.

In the Huntington Library Lieber Collection there is also a diary of Francis Lieber covering the years 1829 to 1860. The volume is in two parts totaling 442 pages most of which are written by hand. The clippings in the main are from newspapers. One part of this *Commonplace Book* begins at the front and the other at the end headed for the center. The former has entries of the years 1829 to 1839; the latter, to 1860.

In the former, the surprising features for the purpose of discovering the relation between Lieber and Hegel-Germany are that references to Germany indicate no special love and devotion on Lieber's part and that in this entire section items referring to Hegel, Kant, Fichte, Schelling, are conspicuous by their absence. Moreover, neither German metaphysics nor German idealism is extolled as in the "Lieber" essay and in the covering letter. By the way, the Perry biography of Lieber has no reference to Kant, Fichte, Schelling, or Hegel in its index!

Again, in the entries in the other part of that *Commonplace Book* to 1839, nothing appears regarding these German philosophers and no great sympathy for the German way of life is manifested.

In the notes written between 1840 and 1860 Goethe and William von Humboldt are exceedingly popular. Kant is first mentioned in 1845 in a brief and unimportant note. *Hegel is referred to only twice, in 1851 in negative fashion and in 1854 superficially.* Of Schelling there is also a superficial mention.

In the diary of 442 pages, then, extending from 1829 to 1860, the genuine Lieber pays scant attention to German philosophers and German idealism. How this Lieber could have composed the covering letter to Crafts or the so-called Hegel's "Metaphysical Religion" therefore becomes an extraordinary enigma.

What alarms the student of the "Lieber" essay even more is that "Lieber" could praise Hegel so superlatively since Hegel himself, referring to his own lectures, remarked: "Only one of my pupils understood me, and he misunderstood me." [28] Francis Lieber was not that pupil.

To permit the Francis Lieber of history to remain the author of the "Lieber" essay published in the Haushalter volume of 1936, after a survey of the data presented in this chapter, would signify another American literary tragedy of serious consequences.

10

The "Lieber" Essay Depends upon "Science and Health"

To refute the accusation of plagiarism from the "Lieber" essay made against Mrs. Eddy by Walter M. Haushalter, it must be shown that the handwriting in the essay and in the covering letter is not that of Francis Lieber, that the covering letter is so self-contradictory that it must be regarded as fictional, that the "Lieber" essay was not composed by Francis Lieber, and that the note on its title page was not written by Mrs. Eddy.

All these counts in the indictment have now been successfully refuted. But there is one final point in the indictment, namely, that of the verbal dependence of *Science and Health* upon "The Metaphysical Religion of Hegel." This count is crucial. There is an intimate relationship between the two documents. Either "Lieber" borrowed from *Science and Health* or the latter borrowed from "Lieber." The former can be shown to have been the case. The striking similarities between the phraseology of the essay and of *Science and Health* are due to literary theft by the writer of the "Lieber" essay, whoever he was.

In the course of uncovering the many historical contradictions and inconsistencies between statements in the covering letter and in the essay and the known facts in the life of Francis Lieber, it has been pointed out over and over again that Christian Science does not owe its origin to German idealism in general nor to Hegel in particular. That the nine pages of the essay could form the basis of *Science and Health* borders on the ridiculous. An examination of the situation in detail will confirm this general conviction.

Since the "Lieber" essay has been shown to be post-1865 and indeed will be shown to be post-1887 in the findings, it is a work of supererogation to add the meticulous demonstration of forgery which follows. This "meritorious act in excess of the demands of duty" is not necessary to demonstrate the falsity of the title of the Haushalter publication. It does have value in supplementing the established historical facts with several instances of verbal dependence of "Lieber" upon *Science and Health*. Thus, the non-Lieber handwriting, the historical contradictions, the dependence of the "Lieber" essay upon post-Lieber publications, the secondary nature of the alleged quotes from *Science and Health*, and Francis Lieber's real views on Hegel based on his own letters, diaries, and life unite to present a rather solid refutation of the counts in the Haushalter indictment.

Of the twelve pages in "The Metaphysical Religion of Hegel," less than nine pages, less than 400 lines, are immediately concerned with Hegel. Around 150 lines are alleged to consist of short quotes from Hegel's four treatises: *Aesthetik, Wissenschaft der Logik, Philosophie der Religion,* and *Philosophie der Geschichte.* The remainder is "Lieber" filler-commentary, apology, and polemic with no claim of direct derivation from Hegel.

Allegations of plagiarism become absurd when the authors let Mrs. Eddy jump from page 333 of *Science and Health* to page 473 for her next sentence, then to page 332; from page 475 to page 71 to page 472.[1] Would it not have been so much easier for the real author of the "Lieber" essay to have copied from a large book like *Science and Health* than for the author of the latter to have built her system of faith around the 150 lines of quotes from "Hegel?"

The alarming defect from the point of view of the editors of the little volume is that they did not discover that not one of the over 25 parallels quoted from *Science and Health* and the "Lieber" document on pages 23 to 28, 33 f. and 37 to 41, is found in the Hegel quotations of the "Lieber" essay.

And of the 121 "parallel" quotes (single or several) collected with the aid of *Christian Science Concordances* in the footnotes, pages 72 to 112, only 31 per cent are even based on *direct Hegel material.*

Hence, the case for borrowings of Hegel materials is certainly in default. One could hardly charge any "purloiner" with "purloining" from *Hegel* as far as the "Lieber" essay is concerned. It would more properly be "purloining" *from the concealed author of the essay.* There certainly is no purloining *from Hegel* demonstrated in the Haushalter study. The title of the book is a misnomer.

In "The Metaphysical Religion of Hegel" there may be almost fifty quotations allegedly from Hegel, many of them coming to only a sentence or two. There are only some 10 quotes of more than 50 words.

On pages 35 f., Haushalter has a long quotation repeated from pages 73 to 75 which he accuses Mrs. Eddy of embodying in her First Edition of *Science and Health* at pages 160 f. *Now the peculiar thing about this elaborate quotation is that it does not contain a single phrase quoted from Hegel.* Haushalter is quoting from the ghost writer, not from Hegel at all, and yet attempts to demonstrate that Mrs. Eddy is purloining from *Hegel!*

On pages 37 to 41 there are 19 quotes which are assumed to show that the First Edition of *Science and Health* quoted from Hegel. But again these quotations are not Hegelian materials.[2] They derive from the ghost writer or ghost writers!

On further study, the pattern that begins to emerge is that for actual quotations from Hegel parallels cannot be discovered in *Science and Health.* What now amazes the student is the extreme paucity of citations by the editor for alleged parallels between actual Hegelian sentences and sentences in *Science and Health.* The editor passes by many of the Hegelian statements entirely. The title of the book becomes more defective thereby.

A sampling of ten alleged Hegelian passages to test correspondence to cited *Science and Health* passages yielded these results:

Alleged Hegelian Quotes	*Haushalter Parallels*
1. P. 77. All that is has truth only when it is a definite existent Idea. The Idea is the only true real...	1. Cites from alleged parallels from the current edition of *Science and Health* with the help of "the Concordances" (page 76) but not one corresponds.
2. P. 77. The final Idea is Mind, Spirit...	2. Four alleged parallels, not one corresponds.
3. P. 78. The Idea is made real in the body and the Spirit...	3. The Hegel quote is 8 lines and only one alleged parallel is

Alleged Hegelian Quotes	*Haushalter Parallels*
	found. It does not at all correspond. Something went wrong with the "Concordances" which "reveal some 340 references to 'idea' and 'ideal'..." Well, what of it?
4. P. 80. The one absolute Reality is God alone...	4. Only one alleged parallel. Here it is: "It is objected to Christian Science that it claims God as the only absolute Life and Soul and man to be His idea,—that is, His image."
5. P. 80. God is Creator and in this is His character as Logos...	5. Only one alleged parallel is cited and, as a parallel, is sheer nonsense.
6. P. 83. Truth is identity, the idealism which is immediate, the highest category for religion and all other mental formations.	6. Only one parallel cited. It does not at all correspond.
7. P. 86. The Holy Spirit is eternal Love, the sureness of identity. Eternal Ideas are expressed in Christianity as the Divine Trinity, the Triune God.	7. Only one parallel cited. It contains 63 words. There is no correspondence.
8. P. 90. The Ego holds a compound of separate ideas...	8. Two parallels are cited. Correspondence limited to appearance of word "compound" but different context.
9. P. 94. Evil is felt as pain. It is a negative which must be resolved into negativity...	9. Only one parallel is cited: "Evil is self-assertive. It says: 'I am a real entity, overmastering good.'" Where is there any correspondence?
10. There are five alleged quotations from Hegel covering 26 lines. For only one can an alleged parallel be found. Here is a portion of the quote (p. 99): "In organic life the external we see is only an external by which the inward becomes visible..."	10. Of the four parallels cited, not one even remotely corresponds. The overworked Concordances could only yield "externalized" for "external."

114

Let us now take selected passages from Haushalter for comparison with the 1875 and 1881 editions of *Science and Health*:

Haushalter Book	1875 Edition of Science and Health	1881 Edition of Science and Health
1. P. 88 (24) That Spirit propagates matter or matter is Spirit, is morally impossible. Hegel repudiates the thought in the following words: "With matter we are at once face to face with an abstraction and it may be declared there is no matter."	1. P. 264:13-14 That Spirit propagates matter, or matter Spirit, is morally impossible; science repudiates the thought, and personal sense alone, must father it, because it is unnatural, unreal, and impossible.	1. Vol. II 145:30-32 Science repudiates such a thought; and the self-evident falsity of material sense must father it, because it is unnatural, impossible, and unreal.

Note that there is no similarity between the alleged quote from Hegel and the parallel passages in either edition of *Science and Health*. The identity of words is again non-Hegelian material.

2. P. 87 (24) Properly there is no physical science. The Principle of science is God, Intelligence and not matter. Therefore science is spiritual, for God is Spirit and the Principle of the universe and man. We learn from Hegel that Mind is universal the first and only cause of all that really is.	2. P. 10:27 to 11:4 There is no physical science, the Principle of science is God, Intelligence, and not matter; therefore, science is spiritual, for God is Spirit and the Principle of the universe and man. We learn from science mind is universal, the first and only cause of all that really is; also, that the real and unreal constitute what is, and what is not; that the real is Spirit, which is immortality, and the	2. Vol. I 14:2-13 There is no physical science. *All science proceeds from a Divine Intelligence*: It cannot be human, and is not a law of matter, for matter is not a law-giver. Science is an emanation of Mind: it has a spiritual and not a material origin, and is a divine utterance, the comforter that leadeth into all truth. We learn from divine science that the unerring and eternal Mind is omnipotent

Haushalter Book	*1875 Edition of* *Science and Health*	*1881 Edition of* *Science and Health*
	unreal matter, or mortality.	and omnipresent, a universal cause and the only Creator, and there is no other causation. He a l o n e creates the real and it is good; therefore evil, being t h e opposite o f good, is unreal, and cannot be the product of God.

Notice that this is not even an alleged quote from Hegel. Observe the "properly" as the beginning of the statement, the period after "matter" instead of semicolon; the failure to paragraph at "we," the introduction of "Hegel" for "science": the period after "is" instead of semicolon.

3. P. 85 (37)	3. P. 212:7-10	3. Vol. I, 116:9-14
Beauty is also eternal. The beauty of matter p a s s e s a w a y fading at length into decay and ugliness. But beauty itself is a thing of Life exempt from age or decay and to be this it must be a thing of Spirit.	Beauty is eternal; but the beauty of matter passes away, fading at length into decay and ugliness. Custom, habit, opinions a n d beliefs form the transient standard of material beauty; but beauty is a thing of Life, exempt from age or decay, and to be this it must be a thing of Spirit.	Beauty, as well as truth, is eternal, but the beauty of material things passes away, as fading and fleeting as all material beliefs. Custom, education, and fashion form the transient standard of mortal beauty; but immortality, exempt from age or decay, has a beauty of its own that belongs to Spirit.

Observe that this is not a quotation from Hegel. It is the ghost writer speaking. He omits twelve words from *Science and Health* and turns a lower-case "b" in "but" into a capital "But" and adds "also" in the first line and "itself" in the seventh and substitutes a period for a semicolon or comma after *eternal*, omitting a comma after *away*.

How could Mrs. Eddy have expanded not Hegel but the ghost writer by twelve words?

4. P. 78 (33)	4. P. 71:4-10	4. Not Found
These Ideas of God never amalgamate but retain their distinct identities, and are controlled only by the Principle that evoked them. The mineral, vegetable, and animal kingdoms have their distinct identities, wherein one does not create or control the other but all are created and controlled by God, Spirit.	The ideas of God never amalgamate, but retain their distinct identities and are controlled only by the Principle that evoked them. The mineral, vegetable and animal kingdoms have their distinct identities, wherein one creates not or controls the other, all are created and controlled by God.	

This again is not a quotation from Hegel but the writer's own statement. There are differences in wording too and an omission.

5. P. 107 (39)	5. P. 310:29 and 24:27-28	5. Vol. II, P. 188:24-26
The efficacy of the crucifixion of Jesus is the truth it demonstrated *of the power of Spirit over matter, sin, and death.*	The efficacy of the crucifixion of Jesus is the *practical* Truth it demonstrated *for our understanding, and that ultimately will deliver mankind from sickness,* sin and death. [The efficacy of the crucifixion lay in the practical affection and goodness it demonstrated for mankind.]	The efficacy of the crucifixion of Jesus is the *practical* Truth it demonstrates *for our understanding, which delivers mankind from sickness,* sin, and death.

Again, this is not a quotation from Hegel but a statement by the author of the essay on Hegel. The context in *Science and Health* with its additional words and especially with the additional word "practical" makes the two statements, the one by the author and the other in *Science and Health* utterly different and directs attention to the fundamental difference between Hegel and Mrs. Eddy, namely, the theoretical emphasis in the former and the "primacy of life" emphasis in the latter. This was the discovery of Mrs. Eddy.

6. P. 80 (39)	6. P. 229:15-20	6. Vol. II, 106:15-22
That man epitomizes the universe, and is the body of God is apparent not only from the logic of truth but in the phenomenon before the spiritual senses.	That man epitomizes the universe, and is the body of God, is apparent *to me* not only from the logic of Truth, but in the phenomenon, *that is sometimes* before *my* spiritual senses, *and which the late celebrated naturalist, Agassiz, saw in his microscopic examinations of a vulture's egg.*	The late Professor Agassiz, in his microscopic examinations of a vulture's egg, gave strength to our conclusions of creation, which mortal belief claims and the immortal idea includes. We had made the discovery in metaphysical science that m a n means more than an individual outline, with mind inside of it; that he reflects the mind of God, the e n t i r e universe, every one of His creations.

Again, this is not a quotation from Hegel but a sentence by the author of the essay on Hegel. Mrs. Eddy's statement is much longer and is personal and conditioned, not abstract. It is her experience, not the general experience of mankind. The ghost writer was under obligation to delete the personal references lest he reveal his source, namely, *Science and Health,* and to delete the reference to Agassiz for the same reason. So he rescues himself by resorting to a quotation from Pope.

7. P. 83 (40)	7. P. 134:19-25	7: Vol. II, 84:12-17
It is still believed in some circles that *there is a separate Intelligence f r o m*	Now to a d m i t *there is a separate Intelligence f r o m good, called evil, is*	To admit aught but the good intelligence lays the foundation of evil, and goes to

Haushalter Book	1875 Edition of Science and Health	1881 Edition of Science and Health
good called evil, an error that admits two powers, namely God and Devil simultaneous. This error is waning somewhat and today his Satanic majesty is not deemed so much a distinct individual as a universal power.	*the error that admits two powers, namely, God, and devil, simultaneous, but gives superiority and all worldly success to the latter; this error is waning somewhat, and today his Satanic majesty is not deemed so much a distinct individual as a universal power.*	support two powers, namely, God and devil, Truth and error; and to conclude that error is an intelligence when it is the absence of it, and to attribute superiority and success to error more frequently than Truth.

Notice again that this is not a quotation from Hegel. There is only partial identity. The ghost writer has made several changes in style and in punctuation, omitting an entire clause but retaining "simultaneous" instead of correcting it to "simultaneously."

8. P. 102 (40)	8. P. 52:32-53:4	8. Vol. I, 60:1-5
Materialism supposes body and soul one for a period, until separated by a temporary law of divorcement, to come together again at some uncertain future *day* and in a manner unknown. *This* is even less logical than annihilation.	The so-called laws material, presuppose body and Soul one for a period, until separated by a temporary law of divorcement to come together again at some uncertain future, and in a manner *wholly* unknown; which is even less logical than annihilation.	If Soul and its expression, called man, are united only for a period, and then separated by a temporary law of divorcement, to come together again at some uncertain time, and in a manner wholly unknown, we are left without a single proof of immortality.

Notice, again, that is is not a quotation from Hegel. There are four different words in the ghost writer's statement. He omits six words in the Christian Science statement and alters punctuation. By omitting "wholly" he tones down Mrs. Eddy's statement and by altering her "presupposes" into "supposes" turns the sentence into nonsense. In addition "materialism," of course, does not at all believe in what follows. This is quite an error and proves the priority of the statement in *Science and Health*.

Some of the alleged plagiarisms in the Haushalter study are indeed farfetched. For example, "all that is has truth only when it is a definite existent Idea" (W.M.H., 77) compared with "man is idea, the image of Love" (*Science and Health*, 475:13, 14). Or, "Nature is set up as a creation of the Idea by Mind" (W.M.H., 77) compared with "Nature voices natural, spiritual law and divine Love, but human belief misinterprets nature" (*Science and Health*, 240: 1, 2). And to add further nonparallel passages as the author does is an admission of nonparallelism and uncritical use of the Concordance which was furnishing the clues. It is a homiletician at work.

Advancing now to an examination of what may be regarded as prize "borrowing," let us sample page 28 (quoting from page 87, page 85 being error to the editor). Out of twenty-five lines on pages 87 and 88, Haushalter quotes only five and omits over ten and closes his quote. Mrs. Eddy is accused of stealing five lines, but from *Science and Health*, p. 468:9-15, given as the alleged plagiarism, two lines are omitted by Haushalter. Further, not Hegel but the author of the essay whose name is concealed is again writing here. The two lines in *Science and Health* omitted are unique.

Turn now to page 30 of Haushalter, where some of the lines formerly omitted from pages 87, 88, appear, and *Science and Health*, pages 293:28-31; 127:23, 24; 111:11, 12; 550:25-27, are made parallels. This ability of Mrs. Eddy to distribute quotes in her book becomes phenomenal here!

But page 87 omits four lines and page 88 omits "in the following words." In other words, the context doesn't trouble Haushalter. And the parallels between "Lieber" and *Science and Health* are not exact. We also must note again why he inserted his confusing [and] into the sentence: "Therefore science is spiritual, for God is Spirit and the Principle of the universe is [and] man." He desired verbal agreement with the passage in the 1875 edition of *Science and Health*. Again those passages came from very separated portions of *Science and Health*, pages 10 and 264, and it apparently never occurred to Haushalter that it was easier for the author of the "Lieber" essay to copy from two separated pages of *Science and Health* than for Mrs. Eddy to distribute the "Lieber" passages so pertinently in her book. For all the author of the "Lieber" essay needed to do was to transform "and" into "is" and "science" into "Hegel."

On pages 31 and 32 there is a long quotation from pages 101, 102 of the Haushalter volume, not pages 99, 100 as the text states. This quotation is placed opposite *Science and Health*, page 215:22 to 216:2; 306:13-18; 296:2, 3. Here the same problem appears again, namely, the ability of the alleged plagiarist to distribute her quotes so marvelously! The verbal agreements between *Science and Health* pages 215:22 to 216:2 are simply not there. One doesn't establish parallelism by putting different words with different significance in parallel columns, and the same observation holds for the remaining passages quoted from *Science and Health*.

Out of 106 lines of quotation on pages 30-33 of Haushalter only some 63 could be regarded as parallel to the scattered passages from *Science and Health* referred to, and vice versa dependence even now seems much more plausible.

On pages 35 to 37 the long quote from Haushalter's volume, pages 73-75, appears opposite *Science and Health*, pages 123:4-10; 27:14-16; 122:29 to 123:3; 121:4-6; 121:17-27; 119:27-31. Again, the miracle of astounding distribution on the part of Mrs. Eddy is in evidence, if the charge of plagiarism could be accepted. Again, as in the previous instances, Haushalter's quotations are not from Hegel materials! The distinctive words in *Science and Health* such as astrography, Copernicus, Kant, Hegel, materialism, Ptolemaic, metaphysics, do appear in "Lieber." The arguments have a different slant. In the case of the *Science and Health* "parallel," 121:17-27, eleven lines, seven are omitted and they are pertinent. Finally, the parallelism is general, not exact.

Thus far, it is more plausible to assume that the author of the "Lieber" essay quoted from *Science and Health* than that Mrs. Eddy quoted from the "Lieber" essay. What is definitely settled is that under no circumstances may it be assumed that *Science and Health* depends upon the concealed author's quotations from Hegel's treatises in the "Lieber" essay. For these quotations are conspicuously absent from all the parallels here used by Haushalter.

On pages 37 to 41 the editor or the collaborators present nineteen closely parallel sections from the "Lieber" essay and the First Edition of *Science and Health*. Their case rests upon these. If they cannot demonstrate their thesis here, they have completely failed. Sometimes there is such identity in the materials that either the concealed author of the "Lieber" essay or the author of *Science and Health* must be found guilty of plagiarism.

To begin with, observe, as so often before, that not one of these nineteen quotes of the "Lieber" essay materials comes from direct quotations from Hegel's works, but only from comment by the author of the twelve-page treatise or homily. *Poor Hegel doesn't appear in the picture at all.*

Most of the passages quoted by the editors to prove verbal dependence here on the part of Mrs. Eddy would on examination prove themselves deficient. We limit ourselves to one illustration.

On pages 38 and 107 of the Haushalter study and pages 312:29 of the 1875 edition of *Science and Health*, we find:

Haushalter Book	*Science and Health*
The time is not far distant when *the* theological views of atonement will undergo *a* radical change.	The time is not far distant when OUR theological views of atonement will undergo AS radical a change AS THOSE HAVE ALREADY DONE REGARDING A BOTTOMLESS PIT, BURNING WITH FIRE AND BRIMSTONE, AND THE ELECTION AND FOREORDINATION OF A PORTION TO BE SAVED OR BE LOST.

Observe that the "Lieber" essay passage cuts a passage in *Science and Health* at change. To do this the *our* of Mrs. Eddy must be transformed into the much weaker *the*, the *as* before *radical* must be changed to *a* and a period placed after *change*, thus making the entire sentence very second rate. *The twenty-eight words following the word change in Mrs. Eddy are so humorous as to constitute the point in the sentence, but precisely these words were omitted by the concealed author of the "Lieber" essay, making his quote pointless.*

Moreover, if the context in which the "Lieber" sentence is imbedded on page 107 be examined, one discovers a great gulf fixed between our sentence and: "Emerson, Channing, and Parker have already reflected the Hegelian religion in America in their Unitarian views of Christ and atonement." This is antithetical to *will undergo a radical change. Will* contradicts *have already!* And the sudden shift from Strauss to Emerson, Channing, Parker, and the Unitarians is explained by Mrs. Eddy's humorous words, "as radical a change as those have already done regarding a bottomless pit, burning with fire and brimstone, and the election and fore-ordination of a portion to be saved or to be lost." These words suggested to the original author of the "Lieber" essay his shift from Strauss, the German radical, to the Unitarian movement in the early nineteenth century in the United States. It was this movement that destroyed belief in hell and the foreordination of a selected few to salvation and of the selected great majority to eternal damnation.

Again, as previously, the alleged dependence of Mrs. Eddy upon the "Lieber" essay turns out to be the actual dependence of the "Lieber" essay upon the 1875 edition of *Science and Health.*

Returning to a passage quoted twice on page 30 of the "Lieber" essay from *Science and Health,* we may possibly discover valid reasons for assuming that the "Lieber" who wrote the essay used the 1881 edition of *Science and Health* as well as the 1875 edition.[3]

Haushalter Book	1875 edition of Science and Health
Embryology affords no IN-STANCE of one SPECIES producing another, of a serpent germinating a bird, or a lion a lamb.	Embryology affords no instances of one specie producing another; of a serpent germinating a bird, or a lion a lamb.

There are three differences between "Lieber" and the 1875 edition of *Science and Health.* "Lieber" has the singular *instance* for the plural *instances* of Mrs. Eddy; spells species with a final "s"; and "Lieber" has a comma after *another* instead of the semicolon of Mrs. Eddy.

Turning now to the 1881 edition of *Science and Health* we find:

Embryology gives no instance of one *species* producing its opposite species, a serpent germinating a bird, or a lion a lamb.

This passage provides us with the missing links. The singular *instance* is here; the needed *species* is here; and hence the only item original in the "Lieber" essay is the comma. "Lieber" conflated the 1875 and 1881 editions of *Science and Health,* preferring the latter in this instance.

On pages 37 and 87 of the Haushalter book and page 28:6 of the 1875 edition of *Science and Health* and Vol. I, 30:3-5, of the 1881 edition of *Science and Health*, we find the following:

Haushalter Book	Science and Health (*1875*)
Hegel's science brings to light Truth and its supremacy, universal harmony, God's entirety, and matter's nothingness.	Science brings to light Truth, and its supremacy, universal harmony, God's e n t i r e t y, and matter's nothingness.

Here the differences are the omission of a comma after *Truth* and the insertion of the proper name *Hegel*.

But Haushalter at page 87 note 51, apparently becoming confused, quotes from a later edition of *Science and Health*, 293:28-31, as follows:

Christian Science brings to light Truth and its supremacy, universal harmony, the *entireness* of God, *good*, and the nothingness of *evil*.

which is much less of an exact parallel than the reference to the 1875 edition.

Now, the essay on "Hegel" has a conspicuous difference from the 1875 version of *Science and Health*, namely, the appearance of *Hegel's* and it has five differences from the quote from the later edition of *Science and Health*, namely, the omission of *Christian*, *entireness*, *good*, and *evil*, and *God's* for *of God*.

Turning to this passage in the 1881 edition of *Science and Health*, we find:

Metaphysical science brings to light Truth and its supremacy, universal harmony, God's entirety, and the nothingness of matter.

Notice that this 1881 version has *metaphysical* before *science*, which suggested *Hegel's* in the "Lieber" essay, *and the latter has no comma* after *Truth* and so agrees completely in this respect with the *Science and Health* version of 1881. Again, the ghost writer of "The Metaphysical Religion of Hegel" has conflated the 1875 and 1881 editions of *Science and Health*.

From our analysis of the sermon of "Lieber," the hidden purpose of its compiler and his homiletical method become clear. He used *Science and Health* as source, and quotes from some accessible Hegelian materials as filler. But what he really had in mind as the theme of his homily was a defense of the Straussian view of Christ.

124

His homily begins with an apology for Strauss by way of a comment upon Kant:

Kant prepared the path for Hegel. In Kant's Religion Within the Bounds of Pure Reason (Religion innerhalb der Grenzen der blossen Vernunft), *he put aside the historical Jesus and founded Christianity on the metaphysical Christ.* Jesus could be a man born according to nature or not a historical figure at all. It did not matter. The essence of Christianity is in the Christ Ideal which lives in every man. The Divine Image, Idea, or Christ was before Abraham, is, and ever will be united with the Divine Principle, God.[4]

In the apparent climax of his discourse, which is actually an introduction to his apology for Strauss, "Lieber" said: "We come now to consider Hegel's doctrine of Christ and the religion of Christianity, which he calls the Absolute Religion."[5]

Then "Lieber" returned to the "metaphysical Christ" of Strauss as his grand climax:

For the rest of this paper we will evidence the principles of Hegel as applied to Jesus by the great Hegelian, David Friedrich Strauss.[6]

Strauss sacrifices the historical Jesus to the Christ-Idea, or Absolute Truth.[7]

"Lieber" finally united Kant, Hegel, Strauss in a closing eulogy:

The suggestion of Kant for a metaphysical religion high and safe above the mere historical and dogmatic was fulfilled in the Absolute Religion of Hegel.[8]

But "Lieber" is still not satisfied with his defense of Strauss. The last "Note" in his essay reads:

The "mythical" theory of Jesus as set forth by Strauss is an inevitable outcome of Hegelianism. While Kant made it clear to thinking minds that Christianity is not founded on a historical Jesus but on a metaphysical "Christos" yet the popular rancor toward the "Jesus fiction" is, as yet in America, a thing to be feared by men in public life. Lieber[9]

Thus this exceedingly enigmatic essay called "The Metaphysical Religion of Hegel by Francis Lieber—'Christian Herrmann'" which seemed at first reading to be a glorification of Hegel has turned out to be an advertisement of the Straussian interpretation of Jesus by way of alleged excerpts from Hegel and quotes from *Science and*

Health plus comments by "Lieber"—a sort of "dissociated personality."

The ghost writer or writers covered too much "metaphysical" territory to give a sound interpretation of the Hegelian system of philosophy. Their own comments increased the metaphysical confusion. There is too little of Hegel and too much of the ghost writers here. As a new hypothesis to explain the origin of Christian Science the "Lieber" essay fails lamentably. It, of course, makes no such claim. It is not a profound dissertation on the philosophy and religion of Hegel.

For almost two decades now this "Lieber" essay has been available for use by students of the Hegelian philosophy; it does not seem to have altered or added to their interpretation of Hegel's metaphysics. So "The Metaphysical Religion of Hegel by Francis Lieber—Christian Herrmann" has turned out to be a burlesque on Georg Wilhelm Friedrich Hegel, not written by Francis Lieber, never seen or handled by Mrs. Eddy, "an adventure into error," which may take its place in American history as such.

The Findings

1. What impresses the casual reader of the Haushalter volume entitled *Mrs. Eddy Purloins from Hegel* most at first is the claim of tremendous research engaged in to produce it. For example, on pages 7 and 8, this impressive paragraph appears:

The research was conducted in leading American libraries from the Atlantic to the Pacific. *No ancient or modern idealistic writings antedating 1870 were neglected.* Jacob Boehme's *Expositions of Moses* (London, 1654), Astrey's *Emblems* (1760), Malebranche's *Dialogues* (London, 1699), *and a thousand similar leads were consulted in the treasure rooms of great libraries.* Now it would be William Adam's *Elements of Christian Science* (Wisconsin, 1850) to be ransacked, or Swedenborg, or Sir Edwin Arnold's translation of the Bhagavad-Gita. Again such works as Ackermann's *Das Christliche Im Plato* (Hamburg, 1835) would call attention. Dusty volumes on Animal Magnetism, Influence of Religion on Health, Mesmerism, Kabbalism, were scanned *exhaustively.* When the libraries of America failed to produce suspected works such as Jane Lead's *Fountain of Gardens or Eternal Invisibles,* photostats were secured from the British Museum. So it continued from Aristotle's Metaphysics to Brownson's *New Views, the list expanding to many thousands of tomes.*

Then one begins to marvel as to why the various authors referred to in "The Metaphysical Religion of Hegel" are not mentioned. Where is Strauss' *Life of Jesus* to which "Lieber" gives so much space in his twelve-page essay.

And when Mrs. Eddy is accused of depending upon "Lieber,"

why is there no footnote at page 92 of the Haushalter study calling attention to "Lieber's," "theft" from Otto Pfleiderer. For "Lieber" wrote:

The treatment of evil by Hegel is on the lines of Baader and the Theodicy of Leibnitz. Evil is negation, the absence of Essence. The negation of evil is finite and not connected with God...

Haushalter has no comment on the passage, except the reference to *Science and Health*, 470:13, 14.

But in 1887 there had been published in London, Professor Otto Pfleiderer's *The Philosophy of Religion on the Basis of its History*, where in Volume II at pages 61 f. one reads:

Krause's solution of the problem [of evil] is quite on the lines of Leibnitz's theodicy. Evil, including wickedness, is negation, in part a simple want of essence, in part a malformation of life... Evil as non-essential has its sphere only in the finite and temporal, it is not to be connected with God in any way...

Krause appears in "Lieber's" essay at page 100: Hegel, Baader, and Leibnitz at page 92. The discussion condemns "evil." The dependence of "Lieber" upon Pfleiderer is plain, since Pfleiderer could not have known the "Lieber," who was not in existence as yet or, to grant an absurdity, at least not published or in hiding. But how could a document composed in 1865 have anticipated the words that would be used by a *translator* of Pfleiderer in 1887. Is it not much simpler to assume that some "Lieber" of, say, the late 19th century was reading Pfleiderer in *translation* in some American library?

The author of "The Metaphysical Religion of Hegel" seems to have been very fond of the 1887 translation of Pfleiderer as may be seen from another example of dependence upon it. The readers will recall how this statement in "Lieber" perplexed us:

God is Omnipotence (*Ormight*), Love, Life, Principle, Intelligence, the Good (*das Gut*), the Beautiful, the True. The Divine Essence is the one highest, unconditional Good. The Goodness of the finite is only in giving form to the divine. (Haushalter, p. 85)

Ormight and *das Gut* gave much difficulty earlier. Both words are not ordinarily good German. They may be mistakes in printing for philosophical reasons or invented. Again Haushalter has no comment except the attempt to associate the passage with *Science and Health*.

But in Pfleiderer's second volume in close proximity to the former source passages, one finds:

God ... is Omnipotence (or Ormight) ... the good (das Gut).
... the true, the good, and the beautiful ... the divine essence is the one ... unconditioned ... highest good.
... Similarly the goodness of every finite being consists in its actually clothing with form in time its God-like essence. (pp. 57 and 58)

The comments above upon the dependence of "Lieber" upon Pfleiderer hold here, except that "Lieber" this time actually copies the odd expressions *Ormight* and *das Gut* from the Pfleiderer volume.

This comparison of "Lieber" with Pfleiderer increases one's earlier conviction that "Lieber's" essay was written long after the death of Francis Lieber in 1872. Research by index is neither difficult nor too dependable nor time-consuming. If "many thousands of tomes" were studied to discover the sources of *Science and Health* and yielded only a recent twelve-page basis, "The Metaphysical Religion of Hegel" not written by Francis Lieber, the majority of readers might conclude that the author of *Mrs. Eddy Purloins from Hegel* was in error. Could there be something approaching homiletical exaggeration here?

2. The second finding is concerned with the ethical implications of this study.

In the attempt to come upon the purpose of this study one discovers items like these:

(1) The purpose of this book is the discharge of a responsibility in a purely dispassionate analysis of her [Mrs. Eddy's] writings in the light of the newly discovered document. (page 42)

(2) Mrs. Eddy in the lucid spots must be the voice for some powerful philosophic Unknown. (page 4)

(3) ... a considerable part of what she [Mrs. Eddy] produced bears her own indubitable mark. But the fact is irrefutable that the chief doctrinal points, the main ideas in *Science and Health*, including the major portion of the "Scientific Statement of Being," are appropriated verbatim from this antecedent statement, the newly discovered Source Document. (page 14)

(4) ... nature imposes penalties on abortive efforts to achieve good through trickery. (page 16)

(5) The shedding of false judgements and the arrival at a dependable understanding of her [Mrs. Eddy's] case will come by a blend of the critical faculty with the fresh factor which these pages introduce into the problem—the scrutiny of the Source Document recently discovered in New England and the tracking of Mrs. Eddy's metaphysics to German origins. (pages 62f.)

From the Mt. Everest of these lofty pretensions one descends the rugged slopes to the valley of unfulfilled promises.

It seems to us that the primary responsibility of the authors was to establish the authenticity of the "newly discovered documents." That was assumed in homiletical fashion. Critical study would have revealed in 1929, a quarter of a century ago, that Francis Lieber did not write it.

Instead of "dispassionate analysis," turbulent feeling has been discovered. Attempts have been made to suppress discussion of the issues involved. Hopes and expectations and frustrations have followed in rapid succession for its promoters.

The "powerful philosophic Unknown" behind Mrs. Eddy has been demonstrated by a quartette of German historians to have been her own *Religious Experience*. Listen to one of them, Victor Weiss, in *Die Heilslehre der Christian Science* (Gotha, 1927, 141-176) once more. He first quotes two statements by Mrs. Eddy and then offers his interpretation:

Those who formerly sneered at it [*Science and Health*] as foolish and eccentric, now declare Bishop Berkeley, Ralph Waldo Emerson, or certain German philosophers to have been the originators of the Science of Mind-healing therein stated. (*Retrospection*, 37)

Far be it from me to tread on the ashes of the dead or to dissever any unity that may exist between Christian Science and the philosophy of a great and good man, for such was Ralph Waldo Emerson. (*Miscellany*, 306)

Now Victor Weiss writes:

If Mrs. Eddy really knew and used Emerson's philosophy, *she nevertheless handled his thoughts freely and independently and partly rethought through his fundamental positions much more consistently to their logical conclusion.* (p. 169)

Christian Science has been found to possess a central unique difference from all brands of German idealism and particularly Hegelianism: the emphasis upon the practical which Hegel did not possess.

Psychology long ago exploded the myth that dependence must be assumed where religious leaders announce comparable "revelations," and no philosopher of standing whom I have consulted admits that "Lieber" understands Hegelianism. Historians have traced the period of origin of the "Lieber" essay to post-1887 times and questioned its historicity.

We may hope that after all this preliminary spadework the true story of the origin of the "Lieber" manuscript may be established beyond a doubt. The law of sowing and reaping is still in operation. The harvest of truth may be in the offing.

3. The third finding is concerned with some strange admissions on pages 43 and 44 of the Haushalter volume regarding "plagiarism." He discriminates between borrowing and stealing from literary masterpieces. Richard Wagner, he says, committed theft in *Die Meistersinger;* Brahms borrowed from Beethoven; Leonardo de Vinci "borrowed extensively." Michelangelo stole from Quercia and Raphael from Michelangelo.

Failure to mention "borrowing" in all the religions of the world, in most of the sermons preached Sunday after Sunday, in the poets, in William Shakespeare, in all the books of the Bible, in the synoptic Gospels, in hymn tunes and popular tunes may be atoned for by the observation: "but where Strauss borrows old things they are created anew, made to flow as with molten fires of rhythm and melody essentially Straussian."

But the author of the Haushalter volume does not seem to realize that back of the sources of all writers are other sources which run back to the beginnings of tribal folklore. So all become the heirs of the past and the future always adds some new touch which permits it to make some proprietary claim.

On his own assumptions the creative ability found on every page of *Science and Health* called for acknowledgement and praise.

Since "Lieber's" essay, a twelve-page affair, admits dependence upon a score of mentioned sources and since hidden sources have been discovered like Pfleiderer and Mrs. Eddy's *Science and Health* with a minimum dependence upon Hegel, why was the Haushalter

131

book entitled *Mrs. Eddy Purloins from Hegel?* There is purloining from *Science and Health* here in the "Lieber" essay, not vice versa. A title such as *Christian Herrmann Purloins from Science and Health* would have been far more appropriate than the present title. That was "Herrmann's" primary mine. This *omnium gatherum* for a twelve-page homily would soon result in an empty church. Pages 43 and 44 could have added to "Lieber's" essay without danger to either.

In the presence of all the borrowing of orthodox Christianity from its environment, one is embarrassed by the innocence of a modern churchman who does not mention it.

The almost complete transformation of original Christianity came in the acceptance of the mythology, theology, and philosophy of the non-Christian world. Faith in a dying and rising Savior had become universal. Christianity became the religion of Europe. The Roman imperial totalitarian setup was adopted by and adapted to Christianity.

The student of Christian theology soon observes that he is concerned not only with Jesus and Paul, but with Plato, Aristotle, and much other non-Christian thought. A very orthodox Christian theologian was accustomed to tell his students that the existence of God could not be demonstrated and then expounded the various arguments for the existence of God on the basis of extra-Christian quotes. So much was borrowed from the Graeco-Roman philosophers that the students' faith in Christian theological superiority was shaken to its foundations. Could it be true that Justin the Martyr was acquainted with Aristotle, that Tertullian integrated the dialectic of Aristotle with Stoicism, that the invading Arian Germanic tribes could repeat the Apostles' Creed, that the church's knowledge of Aristotle rested on Boethius, that the Neo-Platonist Synesius was a Christian bishop, that when no mention is made of the resurrection of the flesh, the incarnation, the creation of the world in an ancient Christian document, it may be a Neo-Platonic tract, that about the sixth century a Neo-Platonist wrote a number of tracts and letters which later Christians regarded as authentic, as composed by a pupil of Paul and through the succeeding centuries were integrated with "orthodox" Christian doctrine, that Aristotle to 1300 was regarded as on the heretics' side and thereafter the orthodox boldly quoted him? Does it have no significance that Irenaeus derived his Christology from a complete misinterpretation of Psalm 82?

That—in the presence of the Christian integration of ancient extra-Christian thought with Christian thought, of the reconstruction of surviving pagan philosophical ruins into Christian ramparts —contemporary Christian writers should manifest such agitation because of variations from four-century-old orthodoxy among the four hundred American religious groups, and go on the still hunt for "sources," merely demonstrates colossal ignorance of Christianity's past. If one does not become familiar with the history of Christianity in the divinity school classroom one faces the painful alternative of learning "who was who and what was what" in the twentieth-century American environment. In the end, for example, leading twentieth-century pulpit orators will yet apologize for affirming the historicity of Cotton Mather's "yours in the bowels of Christ" letter.

Instead of claiming too much uniqueness for one's self, it would be wise to agree with Carlyle, *On Heroes, Hero-Worship, and the Heroic in History*, where he writes:

What he [the spiritual hero] says, all men were not far from saying, were longing to say. The Thoughts of all start up as from enchanted sleep, around his thought, answering to it, Yes, even so! Joyful to men as the dawning of the day from night; is it not indeed the awakening for them from no-being into being; from death into life? We still honour such a man; call him Poet, Genius, and so forth; but to these wild men he was a very magician, a worker of miraculous unexpected blessing for them, a Prophet, a God! *Thought once awakened does not again slumber; unfolds itself into a System of Thought; grows, in man after man, generation after generation, till its full stature is reached.*

4. The fourth finding is that the editors or collaborators in the production of the Haushalter volume have nodded again and again in their proofreading and comments and method. The notes of this study contain many instances. Here, in summary, only a few illustrations need be cited:

(1) The manuscript on "The Metaphysical Religion of Hegel" proves to be a lengthy and learned treatise in the handwriting of Lieber, bearing his signature and his pen name Christian Herrmann. (page 21)

The Hegel comment comes to some nine pages; the quoted passages to a minimum. The essay is not learned, was not written or composed by Francis Lieber; does not bear his signature or his pen name. Because of Lieber's lack of interest in Strauss, the large amount of emphasis upon Strauss suggests the composition of the "Lieber" essay in the post-Pfleiderer age, that is, in the twentieth century.

(2) On page 16 of Haushalter, this statement is disturbing:

...it was not until 1912, two years after her [Mrs. Eddy's] death, that *Science and Health* appeared in the German language.

This editorial comment conveys a very erroneous impression of the influence of Christian Science in Germany:

Mrs. Eddy expressed warm interest in the early Christian Science work in Germany and in 1899 declared to Frau Guenther-Peterson, "I look upon the German nation, as one of the chief supporters of Christian Science." (*Historical Sketches*, by Clifford P. Smith, p. 251) In 1900 she gave a thousand dollars to First Church of Christ, Scientist, of Hannover. (*Ibid.*) In 1903 she started *Der Herold der Christian Science*, the first Christian Science periodical to be published in a language other than English. Though the German translation of Science and Health did not appear until 1912 preparation for it must obviously have been undertaken some years before, during Mrs. Eddy's lifetime.

Popular writings on Christian Science have been in circulation in Germany from the beginning of the twentieth century. As early as 1903, Peabody's polemic against the organization was published in German translation. Converts were numerous. *Before 1910 psychologists were publishing serious analyses of the new religion.* (R.G.G. I, 1580)

(3) On page 20 of the Haushalter volume and elsewhere, statements similar to this:

They [Follen and Lieber] started a "Kantian Society" in Boston in the early thirties, when German rationalism was first stalking through New England and terrorizing the orthodox.

The reference to a "Kantian Society" in Boston Lyceum may prove to be one of the costliest historical errors in the "Lieber" materials. On page 23, it is even said that the "Lieber" essay was "copied for Hiram Crafts, to be read before the Kantian *Group*, Boston Lyceum, 1866." This is another error on the house, since the "photostat" has "Society." After the book was published this "Kantian Society" error was soon caught. The Boston Library authorities have not found such a society. Moreover, Mr. Beauchamp, printer of the volume and mentioned as collaborator, seems to have been so disturbed by the inaccuracy that he engaged special help to discover its existence. The reviser of the original Christian Herrmann letter appears to have nodded several times here.

(4) On page 13 of the Haushalter volume the editors allege that Crafts had learned the practice of healing by mental means from the "Lieber" document and was practicing it in Stoughton, Massachusetts, in late 1866.

As a matter of fact the "Lieber" document is post-1887 (dependence upon Pfleiderer).

Moreover, in the early twentieth century Crafts acknowledged in writing that he "had learned all he knew of Christian Science from Mrs. Eddy, that she had taught him from the Bible and her own manuscripts and that he remained a faithful follower of her teachings, so far as he understood them, all his life."

Crafts is alleged to have carried this "Lieber" bundle to the home of Elder Crane and so on. Since the bundle has been shown not to have been in existence prior to 1887, he could not have carried it to Crane in 1883.

But an ethico–psychological problem also arises here. Why should he have concocted a forgery transforming his beloved teacher into a fraud for coming generations? Why should he add to his guilt by unloading a forgery upon an innocent Baptist elder for much later release "as a delayed time bomb"?

When Mr. Crafts' deficiencies in grammar, vocabulary, intellectual ability are considered it causes one to guess whether the inventor of the "Lieber" essay was not trying humor once more in making him into the ghost-secretary of the ghost-Kantian Society, Boston Lyceum. The loudest laugh must have re-echoed through the ghost-corridors of the Boston Lyceum when its members discovered in 1936 that Crafts was an "intellectual crony of Follen and Lieber" way back there in the eighteen thirties when Crafts was but a lad.

(5) On page 107, "Lieber" is made to say:

Emerson, Channing and Parker have already reflected the Hegelian religion in America in their Unitarian views of Christ and atonement.

Here the editors have no comment but immediately preceding this quote, the following appears in footnote 108:

The chapter "Atonement and Eucharist" in *Science and Health* is largely an expansion of ideas expressed by Hegel in the above paragraph.

The "above paragraph" is dealing with Strauss, not Hegel. There is no quote from Hegel from middle of page 105 to page 111. In addition, "this is quite inaccurate. There is not a trace of Hegelianism in Channing; Emerson split with the Unitarians before he had probably even heard of Hegel or Strauss; and Parker, the only one of the three with a firsthand knowledge of German philosophy and theology, was influenced by Strauss but not by Hegel directly."

(6) On page 48, the editor has an interesting paragraph. It reads in part:

Hegel flowered in the Golden Age of Philosophy, contemporary with Kant, Goethe, Schiller, Schelling, and Fichte. Thus most of his sixty years were lived near Berlin during the flowering of the richest renaissance of Idealism in music, literature, and philosophy that the world has known since Pericles. Hegel's works were published in Berlin in eighteen large volumes immediately following his death, in 1832. Shortly thereafter his influence began to penetrate Scotland and England, finding popular outflow through Carlyle and Coleridge. Toward the middle of the century Hegelianism won introduction to America through President Marsh of the University of Vermont, Emerson and Alcott in Boston, and by W. T. Harris, about 1862, in the *Journal of Speculative Philosophy* published in St. Louis, Mo.

But the "Lieber" essay contradicts this. At page 69, Carlyle is made to say:

Concerning Kant, who is the fountain of all succeeding German metaphysics, Carlyle says: "The worth of Kant's philosophy is not to be gathered from votes alone. The noble system of morality, the purer theology, the lofty views of man's nature derived from it have told with remarkable and beneficial influence on the whole spiritual character of Germany." Carlyle and Coleridge are the only English writers known in America who ever in a small way guessed what *German metaphysics* means. If they had gone further they would have found a greater than Kant.

Carlyle and Coleridge never reached Hegel, according to the essay; according to Haushalter, they helped introduce Hegelianism into Scotland and England. Well? "Lieber" and Haushalter must settle this one.

As a matter of fact, Coleridge was more allied with Fichte than with Hegel whom he severly criticized, and Kant as well. Coleridge was familiar with three works of Kant, two of Fichte, two of Schelling; only one of Hegel.

Hegel was not popular as a lecturer (for that matter, neither was Lieber), only eleven students attending his lectures in metaphysics. Falckenberg, in his *History of Modern Philosophy*, gives 17 pages to Hegel, 26 pages to Fichte, 43 to Schelling, and 104 pages to Kant. Possibly Francis Lieber, like so many other Americans, could not comprehend Hegel—at least up to 1866! The appreciation of Hegel by "Lieber" would appear to be *post-mortem!*

In 1924, the two hundredth anniversary of the birth of Kant, 605 German works on Kant appeared. Possibly "the greatest of these" was Kant.

President Marsh presented *Coleridge* to the New England mind in 1829. Is 1829 "toward the middle of the century"? While Marsh "advanced the course of German speculation," Hegel was not involved in his efforts. "Emerson remained largely indifferent to the Hegelian system and Alcott almost hostile to it." W. T. Harris founded the *Journal of Speculative Philosophy* in 1867. The Concord School of Philosophy ran from 1879 to 1887. Alas, too late for Lieber!

(7) The exaggerated and unfounded and completely disproved claims found on page 14 of the Haushalter volume—

The Lieber Manuscript gains distinction as one of the most notable documents in the history of American Letters; for Lieber's summation of Hegel's philosophy became none other than the basis of *Science and Health*.

—require no further comment than to record these facts: all the publicity given it did not make the book containing it a best seller; the monetary value at first placed upon it was marked down very appreciably; it did not become a reference book, not to say text book, in theological seminaries. *Requiescat in pace* in a theological seminary library.

(8) On page 76 of the Haushalter volume, one of a number of similar statements regarding dependence upon concordances appears:

Not only is Fichte's phrase "Science of Being" found as a chapter heading in *Science and Health* but it appears throughout her writings, as 54 interesting references to it in the Concordances testify. The words "reflection," "reflects," "reflections," appear more than 200 times in Mrs. Eddy's book.

A concordance is always useful when properly employed to discover possibly related passages but it may not be substituted for the scientific analysis of the context. Agreement in words or succession of words may not be identified with agreement in thought. Anyone can sit down with a concordance and count the same word appearing in half a dozen columns without making a single valid point. In fact, he may become so satisfied with arithmetic as to overlook the most pertinent data before him. Results based upon an index of the *Christian Apologists* have provided students with the most erroneous conclusions regarding the development of sacramentalism in the early Christian community. Statistics pile up but science disappears in the careless use of concordance.

In this case irrelevant interpretation is conspicuous by its presence and prevented the investigator from discovering that the author of the "Lieber" essay, only recently composed, was actually quoting various editions of *Science and Health*. Internal evidence and context usually outweigh word correspondence.

5. The fifth finding raises the question of the veridicality of the Crafts-Crane story. It has so many lacunae and possible contradictions already discussed that one who starts with the assumption that the "Lieber" manuscript was given by Crafts to Crane "in the early eighties," and therefore was in existence at the time of the Concord Summer School of Philosophy, is stunned by the evidence that it actually quotes from the Pfleiderer translation of 1887. Did Crane's memory fail completely as to date? Did the "Lieber" document of the 1880s undergo considerable revision before 1930, including the insertion of the post-1887 materials?

The photostat of the "Lieber" essay gives the impression of much later date of origin than half a century ago. Were there revisions of the manuscript in the possession of Crane in 1929? To which edition of the "Lieber" essay was Crane referring when he made his affidavit? If the source of the existing "Lieber" manuscript originated with Christian Herrmann, who transformed it into its original "Lieber" form? When was this transformation made?

Anyone who has had even an elementary course on the historical origin of the Pentateuch painfully remembers that it took from at least 621 B.C. to the time of Ezra only partially to complete it—not to mention the centuries of tradition behind this canonization of the "five books of Moses." So, back of the little twelve-page "Lieber" document alleged to have originated in 1865 there is evidence of late nineteenth-century emergence of a fragment of its material and of its expansion by the twentieth-century scribes until one begins to surmise that its present form may have taken shape at the earliest just prior to the negotiations between Crane and Haushalter in the late 1920s. Maybe chemistry could give a final answer to some of these questions. In this case, D. N. Carvello's *Forty Centuries of Ink* and *Chemistry and Manufacture of Writing and Printing Inks* might prove valuable.

Let us now return to the puzzling words *Ormight* and *das Gut* discussed in the first finding and found on page 85 of Haushalter's book.

To read the sentence containing the words gives the impression that "Lieber" is paraphrasing or translating a passage of Hegel. But he is not. "Lieber's" source was the Allan Menzies translation into English of Dr. Otto Pfleiderer's *The Philosophy of Religion on the Basis of its History*, II (London, 1887). It was translated in four volumes by Alexander Stewart and Allan Menzies and published in London, 1886-1888. Its German title in the third edition (1896) was *Religionsphilosophie auf geschichtlicher Grundlage*.

In the third section, Pfleiderer discusses "The Speculative Philosophy of Religion": Johann Gottlieb Fichte, Friedrich Ernst Daniel Schleiermacher, Friedrich Wilhelm Joseph von Schelling, Franz von Baader, Karl Christian Friedrich Krause, and Georg Wilhelm Friedrich Hegel.

Now, on page 386 of the German edition, discussing Krause, *not Hegel*, Pfleiderer writes:

Das Wesentliche, so fern es im Leben dargestellt wird, ist das GUTE, und so fern es das in der Zeit gebildete Bleibende ist, das GUT.

The English translator (page 57), attempting to represent Pfleiderer's interpretation of Krause, renders:

The essential, in so far as it is set forth in life, is the good, to be approved (*das Gute*), and so far as it is the permanent formed in time, the good (*das Gut*).

Attempting to make a distinction between the two kinds of "the good," *das Gut* has been turned to philosophical advantage. "Lieber" copies Menzies, the translator, even to the extent of parentheses and italics, but slipped up by not also copying: (*das Gut*)! He has destroyed the Krause context.

On page 388 of the German edition, still discussing Krause, *not Hegel*, Pfleiderer writes:

Als die unendliche Zeitliche Ursache des Lebens oder als Thaetigkeit der zeitlichen Verwirklichung seines unendlichen Vermoegens ist Gott die eine unendliche und unbedingte Kraft und Macht, welche so fern sie alle endliche Kraft in sich enthaelt, Allmacht (oder "Ormacht") ist, so fern sie aber zu deiser wie das Begruendende zum Begruendeten sich verhaelt, Urmacht heisst ...

The English translation (on page 58) renders this passage:

As the infinite cause of life in time, or as actively realizing in time his infinite resources, God is the one infinite unconditioned force and might, which, inasmuch as it contains in itself all finite power, is omnipotence (or *Ormight*) but viewed in its relation to the latter as cause to effect may be called First power.

Here the English translator misses out a little. The German text wishes to show decisively that Krause has invented a philosophical term, so it prints: (*oder "Ormacht"*). The English translator use parenthesis and "or" but slips on the quotes enclosing *Ormight*, the invented word. Krause's word *Ormacht* should not have been translated at all but transliterated as *Ormacht*. Then the English reader would have recognized at once that he was dealing with a philosophical term used by Krause. It is a rather parallel mistake to that made by those translators of the Bible who render *Yahweh* as *Lord* and so on, instead of retaining the original by substituting *transliteration* for attempted, indeed impossible, *translation* of Y H W H.

Stumbling "Lieber" not only fails to correct his 1887 English source into Pfleiderer's own plainly printed *Ormacht* but copies the impossible English word *Ormight* and, not satisfied with this boner, assigns a Krause term to Hegel by at least implication, although on page 100 he has that sentence on Krause. But "Lieber" thus left permanently on record that "his" essay of "1865" was written subsequent to 1887.

And would it not be fair to assume on the basis of these data that "Lieber's" interest in Kant, Fichte, Schelling, Baader, Krause, Hegel himself, the emphasis upon Copernicus, Strauss, Carlyle, Leibnitz, Caird, derives from Pfleiderer rather than from the reading of Hegel in German and his own original translation of the four Hegelian writings quoted on page 76?

Finally, the ghastly *Ormight* blunder eliminates Francis Lieber from any and all association with the "Lieber" essay. Friedrich Krause was a German purist and this bent had such humorous aspects in the speculative philosophy of religion that every German of Krause's period was thoroughly familiar with the student laughter and joking heard in the philosophical corridors at Krause's expense. It was Friedrich Krause who "Germanized all foreign words in a spirit of exaggerated purism and also coined new verbal roots like MAEL, ANT, OR OM." Not yet satisfied, Krause actually sometimes proposed over twenty letter combinations to interpret his heavy theological thought, combinations like VEREINSELBGANZWESENINNESEIN, OROMLEBSELBSTSCHAUEN, excelled only by the contemporary German word for "jeep" or the earlier KONSTANTINOPOLITANISCHERPFEIFENSACKDUDELMACHERGESELLE.

The historical Lieber would certainly have added his best historical pun at this point instead of quoting the English translator's *verbal* rendering of *Ormacht* by *Ormight*. Thus the copying of his English source with its distinctive *Ormight* instead of Pfleiderer's *Ormacht* has been the clue to the invention of Francis Lieber as the author of "Lieber's" essay of 1865.

Does not all this reduce "Lieber" to a rather fifth-rate late nineteenth-century or early twentieth-century copyist? Yes, "The Metaphysical Religion of Hegel" was *copied!* but *not for Hiram Crafts by Francis Lieber.*

With the "Lieber" of the essay alive decades after 1872 and reading Pfleiderer's *Philosophy of Religion,* one wishes he might have perused the essay on Hegel, II, pages 78-116, and underscored passages like these:

Hegel's weakness is that he apprehends this development [world] only as an ideal, logical one, which accordingly is to be built up by pure notional dialectic. (page 80)

But great as was Hegel's insight in discerning in every part of the religious process, in small and great alike, the development of reason, *he yet made a great mistake* in introducing into this field also a new logical development, and theoretical processes of consciousness. He thus missed from the first the right point of view for the understanding of the specifically religious element; the fact was overlooked that religion springs from the heart, and not, like science, from the head. (page 81)

Thus he would have come upon the essential difference between Hegel and *Science and Health,* which has been so brilliantly described by Victor Weiss and Karl Holl: the primacy of the practical.

6. The sixth finding is concerned with established facts.

In 1936, there was published in Boston, Massachusetts, a slim book entitled *Mrs. Eddy Purloins from Hegel.* The sale was apparently not heavy, since the publisher or his estate sold surviving copies as remnants to a person in Ohio who still had some half hundred copies to dispose of in the late forties. The book was a composite, since various associates are personally mentioned by the chief editor as participating in the publication of the volume. All these have passed on. Some "Lieber" or predecessors of "Lieber" documents existed in the late twenties. Their identity with those in the 1936 publication seems subject to debate.

Our investigation has been concerned with the "Lieber" documents published in the 1936 volume and consisting of:

(1) A covering letter dated April 1 or April 7, 1866, addressed to Mr. Hiram Crafts, Secretary of Kantian Society, Boston Lyceum, and signed by Francis Lieber—Christian Herrmann. (2)

An essay entitled "The Metaphysical Religion of Hegel, by Francis Lieber—'Christian Herrmann,'" (and at the end two notes appear, signed "Lieber.") (3) A title page with the same claims as to authorship plus an N.B. at the bottom of the page alleged to have been written and signed by Mary Baker (Mrs. Eddy).

Not one of these signatures could be demonstrated to be authentic. The dates of essay and covering letter were not written by Francis Lieber and did not originate until decades subsequent to 1865. The existing documents were neither written nor composed by Francis Lieber. Mrs. Eddy did not depend upon them for *Science and Health*. Instead, the "Lieber" essay definitely depends upon *Science and Health*. Christian Science was not derived from German idealism but was "autochthonous" in origin. Every existing religion, of course, contains elements inherited from the long ago. We may be reading a Neo-Platonist tract when we think a disciple of Paul is speaking to us. We have completely disassociated both Francis Lieber and Mrs. Eddy from the 1936 publication. The best American handwriting authorities refuse to assign the "Lieber" documents to Francis Lieber, and the internal evidence emphatically subscribes to this conclusion.

What the earlier history of the "Lieber" tract was is problematical. There were negotiations between 1930 and 1933 between representatives of Haushalter and The Mother Church regarding the purchase of similar materials. The Directors of The Mother Church after careful investigation concluded these "Lieber" materials were not genuine and declined to buy them.

7. The seventh finding involves a personal confession. This study began in 1937 when I first read the little blue book and was amused by the fantastic covering letter. On every rereading it seemed more absurd. For me the handwriting was not that of Francis Lieber, but handwriting experts were quoted as affirming that it was. For a time my interest in the handwriting aspect of the matter waned, for I had concluded that the appeal to internal evidence must settle the matter. No Hegelian scholar consulted would admit that the essay could have been written by a competent student of Hegel. No historian who knew Francis Lieber acknowledged his authorship. Meanwhile a graduate student without my knowledge sent the "Lieber" essay facsimile to a competent governmental handwriting authority. Francis Lieber had not

written the "Lieber" essay was the answer. Thereafter two further students of the problem reached the same verdict. Thereupon I became more serious about internal evidence and in far away Florida began to dig in. A German by ancestry, the German boners attracted my attention. With the Hoose Philosophical Library later available for checking and the Henry E. Huntington Library nearby with its extensive Lieber Collection—and very efficient and eager-to-help staff available and a research specialist ready to run down clues at my call—the lacunae in the study were soon filled in and the loose ends tied together to give a clearer picture of the "story behind the headlines." A large part of that story is simply told in this volume.

Personally I have enjoyed my hobby and feel certain that both the Francis Lieber of history and Mrs. Eddy had no connection whatsoever with the "Lieber" essay. What Elder Crane had in his early "1880s" bundle—if indeed he had a bundle—I still wonder about. He certainly could not have had what was published in 1936. One wonders why his affidavit was not printed in that volume and why his story to 1929 and its story to 1936 were not told there. One misses footnotes and exact references. If there is any contribution to the solution of the mystery surrounding the "Lieber" essay in these pages, my joy will be exceeding great.

As for me, I find no reason to dissent from the judgment of a leading professor of philosophy in a large American university who in a personal letter to me wrote:

I am firmly convinced that the essay entitled "The Metaphysical Religion of Hegel," attributed to Francis Lieber, is a spurious and misleading exposition of Hegelian philosophy of religion. This essay appears to be an attempt to accommodate the metaphysics of Hegel to the basic doctrines of Christian Science. Certainly what is here presented as the essence of Hegelianism is little more than a travesty of the real philosophical insights of Hegel.

At this terminal, the temptation is great to emphasize the damage done to the reputation of individuals and a significant American religious group through these now-disproved charges and insinuations, and I would sign a call for a week of sackcloth and ashes and public penance. American Christianity has too often been guilty of assuming that issues are decided by repeated assertions and much noise of "say it simply, say it often, make it burn, and never take it back" and bring up the loud siren and threats. The twilight of that day is fast approaching, for the general contemporary religious trend is toward the ethical interpretation of religion. Theology does not unite peoples in religion; the ethical emphasis does. The older religious syntheses are dissolving. The focusing points of the new religious ellipse are science and ethics.

The European orthodoxies cannot solve the religious problems of contemporary life and they ought not to attempt to accentuate our American religious differences.

Here, the habit of ridiculing any new attempt to understand man must surrender to "by their fruits ye shall know them."

This investigation, begun almost twenty years ago, has delivered Francis Lieber from the burden of taking responsibility for the comments on Hegel and Mrs. Eddy from the charge of having used them.[1]

---

[1] One further remark may now be added to this serious study in which we have been engaged. After this material was in galley proofs and too late for extended comment, it came to our attention that the full reports on the handwriting of the "Lieber" documents made by Albert S. Osborn and Elbridge W. Stein had just been deposited with the original materials in the library of the Princeton Theological Seminary.

These two outstanding experts, working independently of each other, offer such convincing and impressive corroborative proof of the thesis advanced in this volume in a hundred different ways that the author is now "invincibly convinced" that Francis Lieber is not the direct or indirect inspiration for "The Metaphysical Religion of Hegel."

Notes

To the many sincere historians in this and related fields in the United States, England and Europe, and elsewhere, by whose critical work through the years a hearing for minor religious groups to defend their founders against cheap aspersions has been gained;

To all who through high school, college, seminary years, graduate courses, and decades of teaching taught me historical method and to try not to misrepresent by interpretation the facts in any document;

To all who by threats and intimidation sought to dissuade me from examining these documents by critical methods, thereby compelling me to read them over and over again and write this summary of the story behind the title, the author's thanks are due.

The notes indicate how heavy is my debt to my colleagues and fellow workers in criticism.

Foreword

1. By Walter M. Haushalter. Hereafter abbreviated W.M.H.

In addition to Haushalter, collaborators mentioned in a letter of W.M.H., Sept. 1, 1949, are: "Messrs. Beauchamp, E. S. Bates, J. V. Dittemore" who have now "passed on to the Higher Life." No attempt has been made to trace the various strata.

After the Boston publisher's death a decade after the publication of the book, his daughter sold the remnant, about fifty copies, to a midwestern woman from whom I purchased a copy in June, 1951. The copy appeared to be of the First Edition. There apparently was no "mysterious liquidation" of the publication, and the few remaining copies were sold to one person in the usual way of disposing of unsold remnants. One curious sentence occurred in her final letter: "From now on the price will be $3.50 [original price $1.50]."

2. W.M.H., 21.

3. *Ibid.*, p. 67. The correspondence between William M. Haushalter and the Henry E. Huntington Library at San Marino, Calif., regarding the Francis Lieber materials deposited therein covers a period beginning January, 1938, and ending September, 1949. Among important items is a memorandum by Miss Norma Cuthbert, cataloguer of the Lieber papers: "We have no letter either to or from Hiram Crafts in the Library—nor mention of him in Lieber's correspondence (2550 letters) [see Freidel's *Francis Lieber*, p. 420] ... the style and phrasing of this letter and document [the covering letter and "Lieber" essay] are not Francis Lieber; the ideology of the lecture is not Lieber; and the hand-writing is not Lieber's."

4. *Ibid.*, 13.

5. *Ibid.*, 14.

6. *Ibid.*, 29.

7. *Ibid.*, 76 note 14.

8. *Ibid.*, 79 note 24.

9. *Ibid.*, 91 note 64.

10. *Ibid.*, 72.

11. *Ibid.*, 88 note 56.

12. *Ibid.*, 129 f.; also 66 f.

13. *Ibid.*, 66.

14. *Ibid.*, 17.

15. Frank Freidel, *Francis Lieber, Nineteenth Century Liberal,* Louisiana State University Press, 1947, 418.

16. Frank Freidel, *op. cit.*, 419, judges the Henry E. Huntington Library Collection of Lieber manuscripts to be the "most important single body of Lieber" materials with its tens of thousands of items. Detailed evaluation in C. B. Robson in Huntington Library Bulletin, February, 1933, No. 3, pp. 135-155. These materials Haushalter had not consulted.

17. *Ibid.*, 420.

PART I. THE MYSTERIOUS COVERING LETTER
1. *Some Literary Remains Are Purchased*

1. W.M.H., 11.

2. *Ibid.*, 10.

3. *Ibid.*, 11.

4. Photostat of covering letter.
5. *Ibid.*
6. See Chap. 2.
7. W.M.H., 11.
8. *Ibid.*
9. *Ibid.,* 12.
10. *Ibid.,* 11, 10.
11. *Ibid.,* 12. In the case of the alleged baptism of George Washington by Baptist chaplain John Gano at Valley Forge numerous affidavits by members of the family did not suffice to establish the hoax. In spite of 42 witnesses allegedly present when Washington descended into the waters of the frozen creek for his immersion, the "faith" proved in the end to be pure invention.
12. *Ibid.*
13. Covering letter.

2. *Historical Doubts Regarding the Covering Letter*

1. In the "facsimile" the letter proper consists of only 34 lines; in the printed reproduction, 53 lines.
2. Lieber to Halleck, March 20, 1866.
3. Lieber to S. A. Allibone, Feb. 9, 1866: "Do you know that I am no longer professor in Columbia College? I have been transferred to the Law School of Columbia College . . ."
4. Letter to Charles Sumner, April 9, 1866.
5. Freidel, *op. cit.,* 370.
6. Carl L. Lokke, "The Captured Confederate Records Under Francis Lieber," in the *American Archivist,* October, 1946, pp. 298, 302; Freidel, *op. cit.,* 373 f.: Lieber to Halleck, May 16, 1866.
7. Lieber to Sumner, March 25, 1866.
8. Several pages in a *handwritten treatise,* April 4, 1866.
9. Miss Norma Cuthbert to Mr. Bliss, Sept. 9, 1949, Huntington Library Correspondence.
10. *Ibid.*
11. For example, the covering letter has phrases like "so uninformed are they here [in America]"; "he loves the Fatherland [Germany]." The essay has such phrases as: "we call in Germany," p. 8; "can now be read in English by Americans," p. 10; "good fortune has not yet translated them for American readers," p. 2.
12. Feb. 17, 1832, Freidel, *op. cit.,* p. 82.

13. Lieber to Sumner, March 5, 1866: "all over our America." Foreign correspondents respected this attitude. See Laboulaye to Lieber, March 28, 1866: "votre beau pays."

14. Freidel, *op. cit.*, 420.

15. Sibyl Wilbur, *The Life of Mary Baker Eddy*, 151.

16. Correspondence with Reference Division, Boston Public Library, May, 1937.

17. Page 282.

18. W. T. Harris, *Hegel-Logic*, 1898, p. xv.

19. See, for example, Steffansson, *Adventures in Error;* Allan Nevins, *The Gateway to History*, 119 ff.; Herman Bernstein, *The Truth About Protocols of the Elders of Zion;* Hertslet-Helmolt, *Der Treppenwitz der Weltgeschichte;* H. Windisch, *Die Christliche Welt*, 1935, #7, pp. 297 ff.; Rosenberg, *Der Mythus des Zwanzigsten Jahrhunderts;* especially "Clio versus Fiction," in the *Michigan Quarterly*, August, 1937.

The exposure of the tragic forgery of the Cotton Mather "Yours in the bowels of Christ" letter deserves extended comment. See the Proceedings of the Massachusetts Historical Society, meeting of June, 1870; also paper by Simeon E. Baldwin in meeting of December, 1902; Extract from Proceedings of Massachusetts Historical Society, Meeting of June, 1870:

The librarian, Dr. Green, called the attention of the society to a letter which had been extensively printed in the newspapers, particularly in the South and West. "It was signed 'Cotton Mather' and purported to give the details of a 'scheme to bagge Penn,' on the part of the Colony of Massachusetts. In an accompanying statement it is said that the letter was found by 'Mr. Judkins, the librarian of the Massachusetts Historical Society, in overhauling a chest of old papers deposited in the archives of that body by the late Robert Greenleaf at Malden.' For the sake of historical truth, it is desirable to give an official contradiction to the story, and to pronounce it a miserable forgery. The name of *Mr. Judkins* is entirely unknown at this library; no such chest of old papers, as is alleged to have been deposited in the archives of the Society, has ever been received, and no such person, as the one stated to have made the deposit, is known to the members. The letter first appeared in the Easton, Penna. 'Argus' of April 28 (1870), and is dated 'September ye 15th 1682.' At this time, Cotton Mather was only nineteen years old, which fact alone would be *presumptive evidence* that *he was not connected with any such piratical scheme.* The story was fabricated by someone with the intention of deceiving the public, whether for the purpose of putting its credulity to the test, or for creating a prejudice against the early founders of New England."

Extract from Proceedings of Massachusetts Historical Society, meeting of December, 1902. From the paper by Simeon E. Baldwin on the Rev. John Higginson of Salem:

"A letter has been repeatedly published in periodicals, and even in books, purporting to have been written to Mr. Higginson by Cotton Mather under date of September 15, 1682. In this it is stated that the General Court of Massachusetts had given secret orders to waylay the 'Welcome' in which Wm. Penn had set sail for Philadelphia, and capture him and his company with a view of selling them as slaves at Barbadoes. As this was the year when the Colony was trembling for its charter, one of the reasons for attacking which was its laws against the Quakers, and had sent agents to London to plead its cause before the Privy Council, the adoption of such an order, were there no other reason, would have been simply impossible. I refer to this clumsy forgery only as the smoke of a real fire."

Levering, *History of the Levering Family*, 68; E. D. Neill, *English Colonization of America*, 307; the Easton (Penn.) *Argus* of April 28, 1870, and the New York *Learner and Teacher*. It was stated by the *Argus* to have been found by a mythical personage, Mr. Judkins, described as the librarian of this society. By the *Learner and Teacher*, it was said to be taken from a copy preserved in the archives of the Quakers in Rhode Island. Mr. Clarence S. Brigham, the librarian of the Rhode Island Historical Society, to whom I am indebted for some of the above references, and the Hon. Wm. B. Weeden, of Providence, have kindly inquired into this and find no trace of such a document.

20. To think that very prominent American pulpit orators were citing this fiction as history in Lent, 1954.

21. Follen to Lieber, Feb. 21 and 22, 1827.

22. *Ibid.*

23. Ernest Bruncken, "Francis Lieber, a Study of a Man and an Ideal." *Deutsch-Amerikanische Geschichtsblätter*, Jahrbuch der Deutsch-Amerikanischen Historischen Gesellschaft von Illinois (Chicago: 1915, Vol. XV), p. 32.

24. Freidel, *op. cit.*, 82.

25. *Ibid.*, 114.

26. *New England Quarterly*, Vol. 15, No. 4, December, 1942, pp. 658 ff., articles "The Minor Transcendentalists and German Philoso-

phy." See also H. W. Schneider, *History of American Philosophy*, 1946, pp. 277.

27. Schneider, *op. cit.*, 165.

28. Covering letter, lines 5 ff.

29. Lieber to Thayer, October, 1866, uses "fogy" and "Reichelberger." W.M.H., 67: "Resort to the use of a pseudonym was made not only in Boston but also in Germany where Lieber wrote under the name Arnold Franz and during antebellum days political articles were signed Americus, Columviensis, etc. Lieber is also credited with the pseudonym The Stranger."

30. Lieber to Halleck, May 16, 1866, upper left corner. Lieber to Halleck, May 23, 1866, writes: "All this, you remember is as yet a perfect secret between us." Lieber to Martin R. Thayer, October, 1866, uses "*Privatissime.*"

Lieber to Thayer, October, 1866: "Who told you *that* tract was mine?" Lieber to Henry Drisler, Aug. 16, 1866: "Do you see the 'Nation'? In the number of this day is an article by me, though not with my name."

31. Sybil Wilbur, *op. cit.*

32. *Ibid.*

33. W.M.H., 11 and 125.

34. *Ibid.*, 66. With the original documents now deposited in the library of the Princeton Theological Seminary, the omitted words in the covering letter prove to be in succession: Otto Krause, Otto, Munich, Munich, Berlin, Krause, Berlin.

35. Paragraph 35.

36. What the inventor of essay and covering letter may have known was that Lieber was an enthusiastic pamphleteer and often had publication troubles even with letters. A touch like this might persuade people of the authenticity of the essay! For example: Lieber to Charles Sumner, January, 1866, asks for assistance in publishing a letter in the *Chronicle.* Lieber to S. A. Allibone, Feb. 9, 1866: "I should like to publish a new edition but such things you know do not sell in the United States..."

Lieber to Sumner, March 21, 1866, writes about an article he would like to have published, but he expects no "leading" New York paper would do it. Four days later (March 25) he writes to Sumner again about a different article: "Articles like this ought to go forth in pamphlet form, but the author is poor and pamphlets do not sell in America, so no publisher will issue any."

The need for publishing a pamphlet is the topic again in letter to

Sumner, April 9, 1866. Lieber says: "Pamphlets, you are aware, are not salable in America."

Lieber to General Halleck, May 19, 1866, mentions a pamphlet again, and Lieber to Benson J. Lossing, Aug. 16, 1866, writes: "I wish my article would be pushed into some diffused paper..."

All these references are to 1866; which may have suggested to the inventor the location of this "Lieber" essay in that year. *The Life and Letters of Francis Lieber* by Thomas S. Perry, published in 1882, and this letter was written after that year.

37. The *New York Times*, the various other New York and Boston dailies published even then the sailings and fares of the *Australasia, China, Cuba, Asia, Persia, Africa* from day to day. The Cunard fare New York to Liverpool was $132.50 and $80.00; Boston to Liverpool, $112.50 and $65.00. See, e.g., *New York Times*, March 31, 1866, p. 7.

3. *Francis Lieber and the Covering Letter*

1. R. G. Gettell, *History of Political Thought*, 1924, 318 ff., 396.
2. T. V. Parrington, *Main Currents in American Thought*, II, 93-98.
3. H. W. Schneider, *History of American Philosophy*, 165 ff.
4. Freidel, *op. cit.*, 154 note 25 and p. 112. Date Sept. 13, 1834.
5. *Ibid.*, 112.
6. Perry, *op. cit.*, 412.
7. *Encyclopedia Americana*, Vol. 6, 218 ff.; equivalent to a column, 1834, Freidel, *op. cit.*, Chap. IV, 63-81.
8. *Ibid.*, 79.
9. Columbia University Press, New York, pp. 646 f.
10. Bibliography on p. 218.
11. Page 165.
12. Vol. VI, VIII, Shakespeare Dinner at Century Club, probably April 23, 1866.
13. Various paragraphs of the "Metaphysical Religion of Hegel."
14. See Part III, 9 and notes 19 ff.

4. *The Handwriting of the Covering Letter and that of Francis Lieber*

1. Published in the *Christian Science Sentinel*, April 3, 1937, p. 611.
2. W.M.H., 342 ff.
3. *Encyclopaedia Britannica*, 17, 991.
4. C. H. Moehlman, *School and Church: The American Way*, p. 144.

5. *Encyclopaedia Britannica*, 6, p. 48.

6. *Science and Health*, pp. 13, 42, 52, 139, 208, 218, 219, 220, 239.

7. J. H. Breasted, *History of the Ancient Egyptians* (1908), p. 273.

8. Lonsdale and Lee, *The Works of Virgil*, p. 9.

9. *Press Dispatch*, Feb. 1, 1945.

10. Jeremiah 36:1-4, 29:1.

11. Ezekiel 40-44.

12. See Charles, *Apocrypha and Pseudepigrapha*, Vols. I, II.

13. *Religion in Geschichte und Gegenwart* (R.G.G.), I, cols. 723 ff.; II, col. 1582; III, cols. 186-189: V, cols. 935-939; bibliography, col. 939.

14.

	The Photostat	Haushalter, 67 f.
1.	April 1, 1866	1. April 7, 1866
2.	my.	2. my
3.	is. .	3. is.
4.	comes	4. come
5.	Otto Krause	5. ....
6.	(from) (on the)	6. from
7.	Otto	7. ....
8.	kindniss	8. Kindness
9.	Munich	9. ....
10.	intollerant,	10. intolerant.
11.	Berlin	11. ....
12.	philosophical	12. philosophic
13.	eight years ∧ age (of)	13. eight years of age
14.	but but	14. but
15.	ship. Keep	15. ship. [New York-Boston boat.] Keep
16.	Krause	16. ....
17.	Berlin	17. ....
18.	Lieber,	18. Lieber.

15. Observations by Mr. Knut Gundersen.

PART II. THE "N.B." NOTATION

5. The Contents of the "N.B." Notation

1. See I, 4.

2. W.M.H., 21.

3. *Commonplace Book*, Francis Lieber, 1845.

4. Freidel, *op. cit.*, 87.

5. Lieber to Sumner, Sept. 1, 1835 (Perry, *op. cit.*, 108); also *Commonplace Book*, February, 1841, where Lieber's language is rather severe against "word-orthodoxy."

6. Lieber to Sumner, April 8, 1868 (Perry, *op. cit.*, 382).

7. John M. Vincent, "Lieber, Francis," *Dictionary of American Biography*, 1935, Vol. XI, p. 238. Lieber to G. S. Hillard, Feb. 25, 1847, praises the Episcopal system as being most useful as observed in England, while the Germans have religion as a very beautiful thing of the finest of philosophies; quoted in Perry, *op. cit.*, 207.

8. Handwritten notebook in Huntington Library.

9. 1858, notebook in Huntington Library.

10. *Ibid.*

11. Lieber to Ruggles, June 24, 1850, quoted in Chester S. Phinney, *Francis Lieber's Influence on American Thought and Some of his Unpublished Letters* (Philadelphia: International Printing Co., 1918), 52.

12. The *L867* is of course the type of error found so often in the little blue book. It should read, 1867.

13.

The Title page in the Photostat	Title-page words in covering letter photostat
1. The *t* in Metaphysical: t	1. The *t* in metaphysical: 𝓣
2. April 1866	2. April 1, 1866
3. "Christ-power"	3. "Christ Power"
4. "Truth-power"	4. "Truth Power"
5. No number for title page	5. No number for covering letter page

The differences between the "original" "Lieber" manuscripts and their printed reproduction by Haushalter come to about 120 when the less significant variations are not included. The general intention of the editors has been to eliminate spelling, punctuation, careless errors of the "originals" and to modernize titles of Hegel's books which never appear in italics by the use of italics, e.g., p. 7, Aesthetik.

The editors sometimes make insertions such as the very unfortunate one regarding the "New York to Boston boat" on p. 68 or the one regarding Pope on p. 80 or the "and" on p. 88.

The editors sometimes fail to add footnote comments correcting the very obvious mistakes of the "Lieber" text such as:

> Photostat 4—"man" followed by the rest of line blank
> Photostat 5—deletion of two entire photostat lines
> Photostat 5—the impossible word "Ormight"
> Photostat 9—(p. 100 H) The most ludicrous of all the German boners in history—13 German words with ten mistakes and impossible syntax

14. Freidel, *op. cit.*, 420.
15. W.M.H., 22.
16. Photostat 9.
17. Various newer introductions to both O.T. and N.T. books give so much attention to pseudonymity and predating of apocalypses, e.g., those of Enoch, Ezra, Moses, Peter, John, that it is a little difficult to understand how any theologically trained student of the past half century could miss the point.

PART III.   "THE METAPHYSICAL RELIGION OF HEGEL"
6. *The Contents of the Essay*

1. W.M.H., 48 f.
2. *Ibid.*, 107.
3. Falckenberg, *History of Modern Philosophy* (1893), 581 ff.
4. *Religion in Geschichte und Gegenwart* (R.G.G.), I, col. 1484.
5. H. A. Pochmann, *New England Transcendentalism and St. Louis Hegelianism* (1948), 79, 64 f., 60, 55, etc.
6. R.G.G., II, col. 129.
7. Falckenberg, *op. cit.*, 590 ff.
8. *Idem.*, 582.
9. Pochmann, *op. cit.*, 35, 45, 65, 80, 89, 93.
10. *Ibid.*, 22.
11. *Ibid.*, 111 ff. "Behind the Concord School of Philosophy which Alcott and Harris organized, there was this hope and plan to bring New England Transcendentalism and the Western democratic idealism together. But East and West merely met at Concord, for by this time neither movement had enough vitality left to launch a major philosophic tradition," pp. 184 ff. of H. W. Schneider, *A History of American Philosophy*.

William Torrey Harris was born in 1835, graduated from Yale University in 1858, belonged with Denton J. Snider and Henry C. Brockmeyer to a Kant Club in St. Louis in the late seventies. Harris recalls in 1881 that his translation of Hegel's *Doctrine of Reflection* "was begun and continued under the auspices of the 'Kant Club' of St. Louis, Missouri, and has been used as a handbook by that club."

Harris had been converted from faith in phrenology by Bronson Alcott and interested in the study of German literature by Theodore Parker. Brockmeyer had introduced him to Hegel. He later boasted that he had read Hegel's *Philosophy of History* sixteen times. In 1867 Harris founded the *Journal of Speculative Philosophy* in which the first American translations of Hegel, Fichte, and Schelling's writings appeared. Harris was an extreme right-wing Hegelian.

Attracted to the Concord School of Philosophy by A. Bronson Alcott and daughter and hoping to become the successor of Ralph Waldo Emerson, he persuaded his friend Denton J. Snider to accompany him thither in 1880. In 1882 Emerson died, but Harris failed miserably to succeed him as leader of the idealistic philosophy. Lacking fire and creative ability, the summer school in philosophy was folding. Harris in 1889 accepted the position of United States commissioner of education, where he long served with efficiency.

Snider had left Concord in 1885. In his *The St. Louis Movement* he humorously relates the story of the school, observing that interest in literature grew from more to more and attendance upon the philosophy courses on Hegel dwindled to about a half dozen. Thereupon William James of Harvard appeared upon the scene and "stole the show." Two Boston reporters were very faithful in their attendance. "The Concord School starting consciously with Philosophy had unconsciously developed its at first unsuspected literary germ into a growth more vigorous than itself, being younger and not so dry." Snider judged that "the final bomb demolishing our philosopher's entire coliseum of the universe" was dropped one day when the Hegelian definition of a hole in your coat was reported by a student just back from Germany to have been: "the partial negation of the totality of the being-on-and-around-itself (des an-und-um sich Seyns)."

Yet it seems that this nine-year attempt to popularize Hegelianism in New England provided the necessary popularizations of Hegel's writings as well as the suggestion to found a ghost Kantian club at Boston since a real one existed in St. Louis. Without nine summers of lectures at the Concord Hegelian cell, America might have escaped "The Metaphysical Religion of Hegel."

It was J. H. Stirling's *The Secret of Hegel,* published in London in 1865, which introduced Hegel to England. In 1883, Edward Caird published his *Hegel* in the *Blackwood Philosophical Classics* and it was in 1886 when Bosanquet's *Introduction to Hegel's Philosophy of Fine Art* became available. The following year Kuno Fischer's *History of Modern Philosophy* appeared in translation. That year also saw G. S. Morris's *Philosophy of the State.*

One wonders how a "great authority on Hegel" like "Francis Lieber" can be so consistently neglected, made conspicuous by his absence in all discussions of Hegel between 1879 and 1887 in the Concord Summer School of Philosophy! Here would have been the most auspicious time for Mr. X to have sold his "Lieber documents" for at least $25.00. The only trouble is that they had not as yet been composed. In the 1880's any bright American living in the vicinity of Concord, Mass., could have picked up in restaurant chatter sufficient materials to compose "The Metaphysical Religion of Hegel." Was Yankee ingenuity and salesmanship at such low ebb as to postpone to 1929 what could have been so readily accomplished in 1880? "In the early 1880's"!

12. The differences between the photostat and the printed Haushalter reproduction are recorded in the following:

Page 1. "The Metaphysical Religion of Hegel by Francis Lieber —'Christian Herrman.'"	Page 71 of Haushalter.
1. by	1. By
2. Herrmann	2. Hermann
3. says =	3. says:
4. charac̅ter	4. character
5. greatest of _∧ metaphysicians _all_	5. greatest of all metaphysicians
6. Religion Within The Bounds of Pure Reason	6. _Religion Within_ THE _Bounds of Pure Reason_
7. (Religion innerhalb der Gren⁄zen der blossen Vernunft),	7. _(Religion innerhalb der Grenzen der blossen Vernunft),_
8. metap̈hysical	8. metaphysical
9. { lives / i/s	9. lives
10. Kants	10. Kant's
11. thought	11. thought.
12. in _∧ astronomy _the celestial_	12. in the celestial astronomy
13. reinene	13. _reinen_
14. Kritik der reinene Vernunft	14. _Kritik der reinen Vernunft_
15. Hartensteins	15. Hartenstein's
16. body,	16. body.
17. intellegent	17. intelligent
18. time	18. time

Page 2 of photostat	Page 74 of Haushalter
1. heavens. was	1. heavens was
2. Freiderich	2. Friederich
3. astronemer	3. astronomer
4. { the / (th/at	4. the
5. 72?	5. 12
6. Vocation of Man	6. _Vocation of Man_

Page 2 of photostat

7. Die Bestimmung des
Menschen
8. Hegel:
9. Philosophie der Religion
10. Aesthetik
11. Wissenschaft der Logik
12. Philosophie der Geschichte
13. and re/lig metaphysics
14. t/he its Ideas
15. { existent
{ fi/xed Idea
16. Idea/

Photostat of page 3

1. Wissenschaft der Logik
2. "Since,
3. { be
{ has
4. . . . .

5. Philosophie der Religion
6. Aesthetik
7. h/im Him
8. explain ∧ mortal man,
       im

Page 4 of photostat

1. Aesthetik
2. Logik
3. . . . .
4. Principle/ It
5. t/he Devil
6. This se]f-sufficing love
7. Philosophie der Religion
8. Aesthetik
9. about 3/5 of a line left blank
after: "a personal man,"

Page 74 of Haushalter

7. *Die Bestimmung des
Menschen*
8. Hegel;
9. *Philosophie der Religion*
10. *Aesthetik*
11. *Wissenschaft der Logik*
12. *Philosophie der Geschichte*
13. and metaphysics
14. its Ideas.

15. existent Idea.

16. Idea

Page 78 of Haushalter

1. *Wissenschaft der Logik*
2. Since,

3. be perfect

4. [Even these words of Pope
are reproduced by Mrs. Eddy
in S & H., 1st ed.]

5. *Philosophie der Religion*
6. *Aesthetik*
7. Him

8. explain immortal man,

Page 81 of Haushalter

1. *Aesthetik*
2. *Logik*
3. [as]
4. Principle. It
5. Devil
6. This self-sufficing love
7. *Philosophie der Religion*
8. *Aesthetik*
9. Not indicated and "a personal
man" followed by period not
comma.

NOTES

Page 5 of photostat

1. Two full lines reading: are immortal. These Ideas of God never amalgamate but retain their distinct identities, wherein one does not create or control the other, but all are created—are crossed out.
2. Logik
3. Philosophie der Religion
4. Philosophie der Geschichte
5. Principle of the universe is man

Page 85 of Haushalter

1. Not the slightest indication of the existence of these two crossed-out lines of the original in the Haushalter transcript.
2. *Logik*
3. *Philosophie der Religion*
4. *Philosophie der Geschichte*
5. Principle of the universe is [and] man

Page 6 of photostat

1. propogates
2. ~~Spiral~~ Spirit
3. "With ∧matter we. . .
4. (Logik)
5. (Philosophie der Religion)
6. Aesthetik
7. rightful/
8. giving to ∧being a higher rank
9. o/f or
10. Logik

Page 88 of Haushalter

1. propagates
2. Spirit
3. "With matter we . . .
4. (*Logik*)
5. (*Philosophie der Religion*)
6. *Aesthetik*
7. rightful
8. giving to being a higher rank
9. or
10. *Logik*

Page 7 of photostat

1. Philosophie der Religion
2. Anesthetik
3. itself
4. Spirit,
5. fails
6. Aesthetik
7. itself
8. (Philosophie der Religion)
9. (Logik)
10. to the describe
11. end of page 7—man must be

Page 92 of Haushalter

1. *Philosophie der Religion*
2. *Aesthetik*
3. itself
4. Spirit.
5. fails
6. *Aesthetik*
7. itself
8. (*Philosophie der Religion*)
9. (*Logik*)
10. to describe
11. end of page 7—man must be most interested in man

NOTES

Page 8 of photostat

1. most interested in man.
2. ⨎
3. Philosophie der Religion
4. Logik
5. Urwahr
6. Aesthetik

7. that ∧ the
    (in inserted above ∧)

Page 9 of photostat

1. inward ~~whie~~ which
2. abstra̶c̶tion
3. Sheer ~~Mastery~~ Self-Mastery
4. (Von der macht des gemuths den blossen vorsatz seiner krankhaften gefuglemeister zu sein)
5. Philosophie der Religion
6. ~~bibl~~ law of divorcement
7. man is ∧ born *(un inserted above ∧)*
8. heaven ~~or~~ and penalties of hell

Page 10 of photostat

1. Aesthetik
2. is ∧ Mind." *(in inserted above ∧)*
3. (Philosophie der Religion.)
4. doubtfull
5. Logik

Page 11 of photostat

1. a̶t̶ printing office
2. is His image

Page 12 of photostat

1. Life of Jesus

Page 95 of Haushalter

1. It is a misfortune that
2. Not recorded
3. *Philosophie der Religion*
4. *Logik*
5. *Urwahr*
6. *Aesthetik*

7. that in the

Page 99 of Haushalter

1. inward which
2. abstraction
3. *Sheer Self-Mastery*
4. (*Von der macht des gemuths den blossen vorsatz seiner krankhaften gefuglemeister zu sein*).
5. *Philosophie der Religion*
6. law of divorcement
7. man is unborn
8. heaven and penalties of hell.

Page 103 of Haushalter

1. *Aesthetik*
2. is in Mind."
3. (*Philosophie der Religion*).
4. doubtful
5. *Logik*

Page 105 of Haushalter

1. a printing office
2. in His image.

Page 110 of Haushalter

1. *Life of Jesus*

13. W.M.H., 74 f.

14. Falckenberg, *op. cit.*, 592 ff. These accusations against Strauss under discussion for years.

15. Knox and Kroner, *Hegel: Early Theological Writings* (1948), p. 54.

16. *Ibid.*, pp. 48-50.

17. Thilly-Wood, *History of Philosophy*, p. 489.

18. Falckenberg, *op. cit.*, p. 597.

19. Freidel, *op. cit.*, p. 154, note 268.

20. W.M.H., 75.

21. *Ibid.*, 76.

22. Knox and Kroner, *op. cit.*, p. 332, and R. G. G., II, *Hegel.* In 1952 a "History of the Lieber-Hegel Source Document" was published. Under "1938," it was stated that the copy of the Humblot edition of Hegel found in the "Lieber Library deposited in the University Library, Berkeley, California" contained "hundreds of marginal notes and inter-linings by Lieber's hand."

Inquiry revealed: "We have checked the catalog of the Lieber collection—which was incorporated into the University of California Library, and have found that there was no copy of Hegel's *Works* among the books listed.

"This library does contain a copy of the Humblot Edition of Hegel's *Works* (1832) and an additional copy of vol. viii (1833) but none of these has marginal notations. There are no bookplates or other indications of previous ownership in the volumes."

23. *Ibid.*, 332.

24. W.M.H., 77.

25. Windelband, *Geschichte der Philosophie*, II, 354.

26. W.M.H., 80.

27. Sibyl Wilbur, *The Life of Mary Baker Eddy*, index.

28. L. P. Powell, *Mary Baker Eddy*, etc., 1930, 59 ff., 285, 289.

29. W.M.H., 82.

30. *Ibid.*, 52.

31. *Ibid.*, 6.

32. *Ibid.*, 82.

33. Page 76, note 16.

34. Falckenberg, *op. cit.*, index and 296, note 1.

35. *Ibid.*, *op. cit.*, 269, note.

36. W.M.H., 100.

37. Vol. V, pp. 701-751; *Journal for Practical Therapeutics.*

38. Ten-vol. edition of Hartenstein appeared in 1838-1839. It was a complete edition of Kant's writings chronologically arranged. There were subsequent editions. The edition of 1867-1868 was in eight volumes. It was the publication of Wilhelm Dilthey's *Die Jugendgeschichte*

Hegels in 1906 that inaugurated the modern study of the development of Hegel's philosophy.

39. Letter of Feb. 7, 1949, from the acting reference librarian, Jean Macalister, of Columbia University.

40. *Encyclopedia Americana*, 1834, Vol. 7, p. 306. Durant's title: "On the Power of Mind to Master the Feeling of Illness by Force of Resolution." In the body of the Kant essay its title becomes "Von der Macht des Gemüths *des Menschen* uber seine Krankhaften Gefühle durch den blosen *festen* Vorsatz Meister zu sein." The additional words are underscored. Had "Leiber read this title he simply could not have made his atrocious mistakes, since in this form *durch den blossen festen Vorsatz* appears between *Gefühle* and *Meister*. This scribe is not a German!

41. See facsimile, p. 9.

42. Could Ernst Freiherr von Feuchtersleben be intended?

43. Falckenberg, *op. cit.*, 329.

44. W.M.H., 92.

45. Pfleiderer, *Philosophy of Religion*, 1887, II, 31 ff., 41, 45, 47.

46. "If God is, whence is evil."

47. Falckenberg, *op. cit.*, 289 f.

48. W.M.H., 95.

49. *Ibid.*, 101.

50. Photostat, 10.

51. *Philosophie der Religion*, III, 111.

52. Knox and Kroner, *op. cit.*, 187.

53. *Ibid.*, 196.

54. *Ibid.*, 297 f.

55. Photostat, p. 10 at bottom to p. 12.

56. See the Haushalter reproduction, p. 106. Strauss did not write a "Letter to Orelli" but to Bürgermeister Hirzel, Professor Orelli, and Professor Hitzig.

57. "Lieber" claims two points of view at issue, W.M.H., 105.

58. Falckenberg, *op. cit.*, 588 ff.

59. 1846 by George Eliot.

60. Translated into English, 1879.

61. R.G.G., Vol. V, cols. 844-846.

62. *Encyclopedia of the Social Sciences*, 14, p. 416.

63. R.G.G., II, col. 1642.

64. W.M.H., 111.

65. In personal letter to author, Nov. 19, 1948.

7. *The Non-Hegelian Character of the Essay*

1. W.M.H., 72, 105.
2. R.G.G., IV, col. 966.
3. Quoted in Durant's *Story of Philosophy*, p. 318.
4. W.M.H., 50 f.
5. Letter to author, Nov. 20, 1948.
6. Feb. 2, 1949.
7. Letter to author, Nov. 10, 1948.
8. *Ibid.*, Nov. 20, 1948.
9. Letter to author, Dec. 6, 1948.
10. Letter to author, Nov. 19, 1948.
11. In a personal letter.
12. *Ibid.*
13. *Encyclopedia Americana* under Hegel, Vol. 14, 68b.
14. Knox and Kroner, *op. cit.*, see index.
15. *Ibid.*, 30.
16. *Ibid.*, 34.
17. *Ibid.*, 57.
18. *Ibid.*, 62.
19. *Ibid.*, 64.
20. W.M.H., 79.
21. Falckenberg, *History of Modern Philosophy* (1893), 487-504.
22. *Ibid.*, 489.
23. *Ibid.*, 490.
24. *Ibid.*, 492.
25. *Ibid.*, 492.
26. *Ibid.*, 495.
27. *Ibid.*, 493.
28. *Ibid.*, 494.
29. *Ibid.*, 495-504.
30. *Ibid.*, 496.
31. *Ibid.*, 497.
32. *Ibid.*, 499.
33. *Ibid.*, 501.
34. *Ibid.*, 503.
35. *Ibid.*, 503 ff.

8. *The Non-Christian Science Character of the Essay*

1. W.M.H., II, 48-64.
2. *Ibid.*, 14.

3. *Ibid.*, 25.
4. *Ibid.*, 41.
5. *Ibid.*, 42.
6. *Ibid.*, 49.
7. See Kirsopp Lake, *The Apostolic Fathers.*
8. John 14, and this is the second century A.D.
9. Mark 12:28-31.
10. Deut. 6:4 and Lev. 19:18.
11. Montefiori on the synoptic gospels and Leroy Waterman, *Religion Faces World Crisis*, p. 128.
12. See Fiebig on the parables.
13. C. H. Moehlman in *Church Management*, April, 1946, p. 8.
14. Leroy Waterman, *op. cit.*, 134 ff., 144.
15. Rev. 21:1-4, 22.
16. Henry Drummond, fellow worker of D. L. Moody.
17. Luke 11:3, Matt. 6:11, Didache 8:2.
18. Adolf von Harnack, *The Expansion of Christianity*, I, 36.
19. L. P. Powell, *op cit.*, p. 103.
20. Victor Weiss, *op. cit.*, 159; see also letter to Boston *Post* in 1883.
21. Powell, *op. cit.*, 113; H. A. L. Fisher, *Our New Religion*, 22 f., note 37.
22. *Ibid.*, 117 f., 294.
23. *Ibid.*, 117.
24. Falckenberg, *op. cit.*, 489.
25. Powell, *op. cit.*, p. 131, see note 9.
26. Weiss, *Die Heilslehre der Christian Science* (1927), Chap. III.
27. George Mahr in *R.G.G.* article " Christian Science," Vol. I.
28. Weiss, *op. cit.*, 175.
29. R.G.G., I, cols. 1575-1582 (Mahr).
30. Karl Holl, *Gesammelte Aufsätze*, Vol. III, 460 ff.
31. *No and yes*, 22.
32. Weiss, *op. cit.*, 176.
33. L. P. Powell, *Christian Science: The Faith and its Founder*, 110.
34. Falckenberg, *op. cit.*, 419.
35. *Ibid.*, 443.
36. *Ibid.*, 423.
37. *Ibid.*, 423.
38. Weiss, *op. cit.*, 159.
39. *Ibid.*, 169.
40. Karl Holl, *op. cit.*, III, 460 ff.
41. R.G.G., I, cols. 1576-1581.
42. W.M.H., 33, 55, 56, 57, 58, 60.

43. *Science and Health*, 107.
44. Weiss, *op. cit.*, 144 ff.
45. Powell, *op. cit.*, 105 ff.
46. R.G.G., IV, cols. 1860-1863.
47. Weiss, *op. cit.*, 172 ff.
48. Henry Steiger, *Christian Science and Philosophy*, Philosophical Library, 1948, 211, 205, 143, 134, 132, etc.

9. *Francis Lieber Did Not Compose the "Lieber" Essay*

1. Under I, 3; see also Freidel, *op. cit.*, 9, 21, 86, 133, 142, 183, 284, 392, 407.
2. Page 9.
3. Index and p. 420 in particular.
4. Page 420 and *Foreword*.
5. In the Encyclopedia, *Leibnitz*.
6. Freidel, *op. cit.*, 340.
7. See Part III, 7, espec. note 40.
8. Freidel, *op. cit.*, 130 ff.
9. Falckenberg, 499 f.
10. W.M.H., 86.
11. *Ibid.*, 73.
12. *Ibid.*, 110.
13. Covering letter, W.M.H., 67.
14. *Ibid.*, 111.
15. 1879-1887, see Part III, 7 note 11.
16. Freidel, *op. cit.*, 416.
17. W.M.H., 104.
18. *Ibid.*, 76. See also Freidel, *op. cit.*, 112, 154.
19. Julia Ward Howe, *Reminiscences 1819 to 1899*, Boston, 1899, p. 210.
20. *Ibid.*, 210. Mrs. Howe was well versed in the German idealistic philosophy because she read it in the German. "Hegel was for some time my study among the German philosophers," p. 209. Later she turned to Kant. "The Kantian volumes occupied me for many months, even years. In fact, I have never gone beyond them," p. 213. These Kantian studies were most ardent around the 1860's, but she fails to mention any "Kantian Society" in Boston, even though she writes about the Boston Radical Club where "radical" issues were debated. *Furthermore, Mrs. Howe had known Lieber from childhood, her husband was an intimate friend of his.* It is inconceivable that Mrs. Howe should be

wrong in her judgments which are based on the diary notes from the time.

George Bancroft also regarded Hegel as a man of weak character. Mr. Gundersen directed my attention to the significance of the Howe materials. If Lieber personally felt as indicated in the quotes very late in his life, how could he have written either the covering letter or the essay in 1865?

21. Laura E. Richards and Maude Howe Elliott on Julia Ward Howe, 240.

22. Lieber to Mittermaier, Sept. 13, 1834, quoted in Freidel, *op. cit.*, 112.

23. *German Philosophy*, perhaps from the year 1835.

24. *Ibid.*

25. *Commonplace Book*, 1851.

26. In Huntington Library.

27. W.M.H., 76.

28. Ward, *op. cit.*, 210.

10. *The Essay Depends upon "Science and Health"*

1. In this section the supporting passages are often quoted in the text to facilitate critical comparison.

2. The citations on 37-41 are in error. Should be p. 84 instead of 82, and 85, 86 instead of 83, 84, etc.; every quote is in error as to page and there are 19 instances!

3. In the 1875 edition, 264: 2-5, 10-14; edition of 1881, II, 145: 23-25.

4. W.M.H., 72.

5. *Ibid.*, 104.

6. *Ibid.*, 105.

7. *Ibid.*, 106.

8. *Ibid.*, 111.

9. *Ibid.*, 112.

INDEX

"Adventures in Error," 150
Alcott-Harris school at Concord, 45
alleged "bowels of Christ" letter of Cotton Mather, 133, 150 ff.
alleged immersion of George Washington, 8, 149
anonymous Babylonian literature, 31
Apocrypha and *Pseudepigrapha*, 45
apodictical, 57, 58
Appelt, 60
Asia (steamship), 17, 18
autochthonous origin of Christian Science, 93, 143
Avon, Mass., 3

Bancroft, George, 167
Barnard, President of Columbia, 106
Berkeley, Lieber collection at, 162
Berlin, 3
Blind, Mathilde, 68
Bluntschli, 21, 106
Boston, 3
"Boston Kantian Society," 11
Boston Lyceum, ix
Boston Radical Club, 166
Breasted, J. H., 28
Bremen (steamship), 17
Britannica, 27
Brockhaus, 99
Brockmeyer, 51

Caird, 71, 105
Carlyle on *Heroes, Hero-Worship,*

and the Heroic in History, 133
Carvello, D. N., 139
catalogue of books, 108
Channing, 49
Charles, 45
Christian Science Board of Directors, 25 ff.
Clark, George D., 11
Coleridge, 49
Columbia, S.C., 14
Columbia University, 14
Commonplace Book, 23, 40, 109
Concord, Mass., 7
Concord School of Philosophy, 156 ff.
Concordances, xi, 112, 138
Congressional Record, 31
Copernicus, 51
copying Menzies error, 140
copyright, 28, 31
Crafts, Hiram, ix, 3, 4, 10, 138
Crane, S. Minot, 3, 4, 15, 24
Cuthbert, Norma, xiii

Davis, A. J., 16
dependence of "Lieber" manuscript upon *Science and Health*, Ch. 10
depository of "Lieber" manuscripts at Princeton Theological Seminary, xi
dialectic, 28, 72, 73, 74, 142
diary of Francis Lieber, 1829-1860, 109, 110

169

INDEX

Dilthey, Wilhelm, 162
Dresser, *Quimby Manuscripts*, 42
Duncker and Humblot edition, 54
Durant, 163

Eddy, Mrs., 25, 57, 86, 119
Ehrenberg, Hans, 75
Elliott, Maude Howe, 167
Elohim, 30
Emerson, 49, 130, 137
Encyclopedia Americana, 22, 61, 99, 164
Encyclopedia of the Social Sciences, 163
epiousios, 85 ff.
error in German, 43, 59, 61, 100, 163
Ezekiel, 32

facsimile reproduction of "Lieber" manuscript, xi
Falckenberg, 62, 76, 87, 92, 101, 164
Feuchtersleben, 162
Feuerbach, 52
Fichte, 53, 92, 93
Fisher, H. A. L., 86
Follen, Charles, 12, 13, 19
Fourth Eclogue of Virgil, 28
Fourth Ezra, 4, 29
Freidel, Frank, xii, 23, 53, 98, 148

Gano, John, 149
Garibaldi, 21
Gettell, 20
Goethe, 23
Gundersen, Knut, xiv, 154, 167
Gut and *Gute*, 140

handwriting of Mrs. Eddy, 42
Harnack, Adolf von, xiv
Harris, xiii, 7, 49, 50, 51, 136, 156
Hartenstein, 102, 162
Hase, 66, 68
Haushalter, W. M., ix, 3, 25, 80, 94, 113, 116
Hegel, x, 3, 23, 34, 52, 54, 55, 56, 73, 76, 102, 107, 110, 157
Heilslehre der Christian Science, 130
Herrmann, Christian, ix, 14, 24, 39
Holl on Christian Science, 88-91
Hoose Library, U.S.C., xiii, 144

Howe, Julia Ward, 11, 107, 166 f.
Hufeland, 60
Humboldt, Wilhelm von, 110
Huntington Library, Henry E., xiii, 9, 109, 148

identity, 158
Irenaeus, 133
Isaiah, 29, 30

Jefferson, Thomas, 27
Jeremiah, 32
Johns Hopkins University, xiv
Journal of Speculative Philosophy, 50, 136

Kant, 74, 102, 103
Knox and Kroner, 162
Koran, 40
Krause, Frederich, inventor of *Or-might*, *Gut*, 139; MAEL, ANT, OR, OM, 141
Krause, Otto, 3, 16, 17, 19
Kroner, 74, 162

Leibnitz, T. W., 59, 62
Levering, 151
Lexington (steamship), 12
Lieber, Francis (the historical person), x, 8, 9, 14, 23, 24, 40, 41, 99, 106, 107, 108, 110
"Lieber, Francis" (fictional person), 3, 12, 19, 69, 103
Link, Herbert, 75
Lonsdale, 153

Mahr, 87, 93, 165
Marx, Karl, 52
Mather, Cotton, "yours in the bowels of Christ" letter, 133
Menzies, Allan, 139
"Metaphysical Religion of Hegel," 10
Micah 4:1-3, 30
Munich, 18
Murray, Lindley, 57

"N.B." notation, x, 39
"New York to Boston boat," 8, 18
"No Duty without its Right," 21
Nohl, Herman, 54